A FINAL SOLUTION

Within a few days we heard from the Resistance. Girls had been sent, ostensibly to pick berries in the woods, while they spied on the home of Schwenke's mistress and on Schwenke himself. They were able to confirm that our "friend" left his mistress's house every morning just before eight and took a short cut through the woods. All we needed now was to choose the day and time, the weapon, and the executioner. We all agreed that the executioner would carry a knife, stab the officer to death, and remove his wallet and wrist-watch, as the attack had to look like a mugging and murder by a common criminal.

I was still in bed when the doorbell rang the morning after these plans had been settled. Franz was there, dressed in civilian clothes. His opening words stunned me: "Olga, you have been chosen to kill Schwenke."

All I could find to say was, "Why me?"

Inside the Gestapo

A Jewish Woman's Secret War

Helene Moszkiewiez

A DELL BOOK

Published by
Dell Publishing Co., Inc.
1 Dag Hammarskjold Plaza
New York, New York 10017

Dell ® TM 681510, Dell Publishing Co., Inc.

ISBN: 0-440-14112-5

Reprinted by arrangement with Macmillan of Canada.

Printed in the United States of America

September 1987

10 9 8 7 6 5 4 3 2 1

WFH

Contents

To the memory of my parents,
and of all the victims of the Holocaust

Acknowledgements

I am grateful for their invaluable help and support to my husband, who encouraged me to tell my story, and who wrote it in English for me; to Susan Egan; to Kathleen Richards, my editor; and to Professor M. R. Steinberg.

H.M.

Foreword

Most of the names in this book are fictitious, but the characters are real, and the events true.

Because these persons or their descendants may still be alive, I feel it does not behoove me to reveal their real names at this time. However, if some independent investigator, say a journalist, should find out the real name of any such person and publish it as belonging to History, I shall be only too pleased, if the findings are correct, to make the necessary changes for a revised edition.

On the other hand, I do not know or cannot remember the real names of some of the people I mention in this book. So if those who recognize themselves in it wish to make themselves known to me, through my publishers, I shall be quite thrilled to get in touch with them.

Helene Moszkiewiez (Olga)
Vancouver, 1985

Introduction

We have just been told in three languages, over the public address system, that we are about to land in the capital city of Belgium, where the temperature is eighteen degrees Celsius under cloudy skies: "Enjoy your stay, and thank you for flying Sabena." After ten long hours from Vancouver, Canada, I am in Brussels at last, the city of my childhood, of my teen dreams, and of my longest nightmare, one that lasted from 1942 to 1944. This is only my second visit in thirty years, and probably the last, though this may not prove to be so.

Fifteen years ago, our two sons came with us. This time just my husband, Al, and I are returning. And this time I have promised myself that I will revisit some of my old haunts to see if they can stir up the same memories and emotions.

I am a little surprised, in this Brussels of 1982, to feel like a stranger, though the streets and people are familiar enough. Today's Brussels is much like any other big modern city, a mix of nationalities, large anonymous crowds, and modern high-rise buildings that contrast with the older, shabbier homes and shops. And cars, of course, are everywhere. They

clutter the narrow, medieval streets that surround
the Grand'Place, heart of the old city; they even
overflow onto the sidewalks, where parking is now
permitted. There is little room left for pedestrians, a
seriously endangered species. Al and I flee to the
suburbs, away from the tourists.

Sol, my brother-in-law, now comfortably retired,
offers to chauffeur us around the city. In the car I
exchange reminiscences with Lily, my sister. First
we go to rue Veydt, to see the place where I spent my
childhood, half a century ago.

I don't like what I see. Our old house looks drab
and seems to have shrunk. Our street is unbelievably
narrow to my older eyes. The sensation is similar to
that of meeting a shrivelled old lady you last saw fifty
years ago, whose features you still remember as those
of a fresh young girl of eighteen.

On rue Léon de Lantsheere, where I hid from the
Nazis under an assumed name, the tiny house with its
enamelled-brick exterior has remained much the
same, and so has the street itself, a neighbourhood of
petit-bourgeois residents that has retained its turn-
of-the-century character, save for a few cars parked
here and there. A huge complex of shops and offices
now stands on the site on boulevard Botanique that
was occupied by the military restaurant where I first
met Al in 1944. As for the famous Café Louise with its
gypsy orchestra, where I met the Gestapo chief and
his assistant in 1942, it is gone. In its place are a bank
branch and flower and gift shops.

We follow avenue Louise, not quite as fashionable
as it used to be, and Sol stops in front of Number 453,
today a well-kept apartment building of eight
storeys. It is not very different in appearance from

the neighbouring apartment buildings, except for
the bronze tablet on the wall beside the double-door
entrance. It serves as a reminder that this was the
Gestapo headquarters during the Second World War.
I should know. I worked in that evil place as a secret
agent from 1942 to 1944, when the place was full of
Gestapo personnel on every level.

My story may seem incredible, but it is true. The
events I recount are renewed evidence that real history can indeed be stranger than any fiction.

From a vast distance now, over forty years and a
continent away, I am ready to retrace my wartime
past. But I am pleased to say that I have never regretted my decision in 1945 to leave Belgium and those
memories for a new life in Canada.

1

Peace and War

Friday, May 10, 1940, began as a perfect spring day in Brussels, the kind of day that makes the most inveterate city-dwellers long for the country. My sister, Lily, who was soon to be married, had planned to spend the weekend "à la campagne" with her fiancé, and I was preparing for a bicycle outing with some friends in the bois de la Cambre just outside Brussels.

That morning, however, just after nine o'clock, the first bombs fell on Brussels, destroying a number of buildings and shattering our plans. That date is recorded in history as the beginning of the Blitzkrieg, and also of the rape of Belgium by Nazi Germany. With thousands of others, I can count that day as a turning point in my life. My particular wartime adventures, however, began with a chance friendship formed earlier, in 1937.

I was sixteen that year, had left school—which I frankly disliked—and was helping my parents run a modest haberdashery in a residential district of the city. Like so many shops in Europe, ours was part of a two-storey house built around the turn of the century. We lived in the apartment on the first floor, just over the shop. Above us lived Mlle Baudhuin, the owner, to whom we paid our rent. She was the daughter of a Belgian general long deceased, a plain-looking spinster

then in her fifties, tall, stout, and always dressed in black and un-
fashionably low-heeled shoes. She was a very formal, genteel lady
who, despite her somewhat forbidding appearance, later proved to be
kind, understanding, and charitable.

Our shop was the only one on the block, somewhat of an anomaly
in a street of small, middle-class homes; these were like little fortresses
whose dwellers, jealous of their privacy, kept themselves to themselves.
Our immediate neighbours were generally aloof, though polite; even
on those occasions when we dealt with them as customers, our relationship remained formal and purely commercial.

In those days the capital of Belgium boasted a population of some
750,000, but despite its size it had remained very provincial and peaceful compared with some other major European cities. The hysterical
and occasional disturbances by the Rexists were isolated exceptions in
the quiet daily life of Brussels. The leader of this small but vociferous
gang of Nazi fanatics was Léon Degrelle, a man who made up in
bravado and threatening postures what he lacked in brains and common sense, a devoted follower of his master and mentor, Adolf Hitler.
At that point, the German invasion and occupation of Belgium some
twenty-five years earlier was almost forgotten and relegated to history
textbooks; its impact on my generation was minimal.

In the fall of 1937 I met François Vermolen, who was later to play a
major role in my war activities. It was owing to him that I found
myself involved in the adventures that I recount here. I met him by
chance at the local public library. I was rummaging through some
rows of books and managed to drop a whole armload with a horrify-
ing amount of noise. I was very embarrassed and flattered when a
kind army officer came to my rescue to help me clear up the mess. He
saw me home that first evening, and from then on François and I saw
a fair amount of each other.

We were both avid readers at the time, and shared a common
interest in literature. I also found him attractive: he was tall and
handsome, clean-cut with well-groomed shiny brown hair brushed
back after the fashion of the day, brown-eyed and of a generally
cheerful disposition. Until I met him I had associated only with
friends of about my own age and background, which was middle-class
Jewish. At the age of twenty-five, François was a full nine years older
than myself, and so he made a strong impression on me. He was
sophisticated and well travelled, an excellent linguist, and of a higher
social class; also his attention flattered my feminine vanity. In retrospect I suppose my own anti-establishment ideas and attitudes, about

which I was quite outspoken, and my kind of tomboy femininity must have fascinated him. I wonder now whether this mutual attraction would ever have led to a love affair, and it seems quite possible to me. In fact, however, it never did.

François spoke fluent English and German, in addition to Belgium's two official languages, French and Flemish. When I once addressed him in fluent German, he was amazed. To answer his question, I explained that my parents, who were Jewish, had come originally from Germany, and we all still spoke a good deal of German at home. François then confided that he had spent three years in a German university; his father, a colonel in the Belgian army, had sent him there to study medicine, but as he did not fancy a medical career, he had joined the army and obtained a commission.

Eventually I introduced François to my parents, who invited him to dinner a couple of times. My mother's reaction was blunt: she did not like him. She found him very evasive. She said he never gave her a straight answer to a straight question, and that he had the shifty eyes of a hypocrite. Evidently she did not consider him a suitable match for me, although she never broached the subject openly. My father, always optimistic, was a little more tolerant, and he even hinted that he liked the idea of being father-in-law to a Belgian officer.

For my part, I did not take all this too seriously, for I had other friends to date and other interests. I was far too independent to feel attached to any particular boy at the time. François and I met on and off during the course of those two years; we were always the best of friends and we never quarrelled, which to me is proof in itself that we never really fell in love.

Then, in the summer of 1939, he disappeared without a trace. When I had not heard from him for quite a while, and he did not show up at the library as he usually did, or at any of his usual haunts, I was at first somewhat mystified and then worried. I remembered that he had once introduced me to an old aunt of his who lived in Brussels —he himself was from Antwerp. I went to see her, but she knew nothing of his whereabouts. Then Belgium became engulfed in the turmoil of the Blitzkrieg, and as I was beset by more pressing problems, François was all but forgotten.

When rumours spread of the first German tanks advancing on the capital in the spring of 1940, there was panic throughout the city. Thousands of people immediately packed a few belongings and left for the coast, hoping to catch the last boats leaving France for England and freedom. For several days my parents argued endlessly about what we should do: stay or leave. Father wanted to stay. He felt that to abandon our home and lose everything he had worked for so hard all those years would be madness. Mother wanted to leave without delay. She had heard from some German refugees about the brutal treatment of Jews in Germany, and she foresaw the dangers for us of living in Belgium under Nazi rule. She felt that the war could not last very long, and that we would probably be back in our own home in a few months. Lily, my sister, whose fiancé had left a week earlier on his motorcycle, was naturally eager to join him at a pre-arranged rendezvous in London, so she sided with my mother. As for me, I did not fully appreciate then the implications of a German invasion and, as the youngest, I really had little say in the matter. I was most concerned about Mickey, our little mongrel bitch, to whom I was very much attached and who would have to be left behind. For her sake, I hoped that we would stay.

Father made the decision to leave when he heard that several friends and acquaintances had already left for Calais days earlier. As we had no transportation he expected that we would walk all the way. He estimated it would take us over a week to cover the 250 kilometres to the French coast. We each packed a knapsack with clothes, food, and a thermos. Mother also insisted that we wear rubber boots, and at nine in the morning on May 20, after paying Mlle Baudhuin an extra month's rent and asking her to look after Mickey, we set off. I can still see the kind old lady, bewildered and concerned, watching us depart and waving goodbye and "God bless you" from the doorstep. It broke my heart to leave Mickey, and on impulse I ran back to give her a last hug and whispered in her ear, "Don't worry, old girl, we'll be back soon."

May 20 ripened into a scorching summer day. The heat, the weight of our gear, and the rubber boots all combined to slow our progress. We were so preoccupied with our discomforts that we hardly noticed that the streets were almost deserted. Two hours later we reached the Willebroeck Canal to find that the bridge had been blown up and we could go no farther. Uncertain what to do next, we lingered by the canal. A small crowd of idlers had gathered on the quay near the approaches to the bridge gaping at the rubble.

A middle-aged man, possibly a watchman, came over to us and, noticing our walking clothes and knapsacks, asked where we were going. When we told him, he said that all the bridges leading out of the capital had been blown up by the army to impede the enemy advance, and that we would be wise to go back the way we had come.

We had no other choice. We trudged all the way back home in our rubber boots under the merciless sun. Every ten minutes or so we paused to seek the shade, eager to cool our burning feet. The return journey, which would normally have taken a little over an hour, lasted almost three hours. When we reached home at last, Father sat down, gave a deep sigh of relief, and said he was mighty glad things had turned out the way they had. I heartily agreed with him, hugging an excited Mickey. Mother was too tired to talk and went to lie down. Lily was in a vile temper. She resented my apparent indifference to her own welfare and accused me of caring more about dogs than about human beings. Name-calling and blows ensued, until Dad separated us and sent us both to bed.

A week later Sol reappeared on his motorbike. He had travelled as far as Valenciennes in France, and even that far inland, he learned that no more boats were leaving for England. He tried to turn back and found all roads blocked by other refugees fleeing in all directions. He managed at last to find shelter in a farm, and there he waited the week for the roads to clear. The news he brought back was frightening: thousands of people fleeing through northern France from the enemy, being mercilessly machine-gunned by diving Stukas; roads strewn with the dead and the dying, some of them expiring from sheer thirst and exhaustion; and general pandemonium throughout the countryside. We realized how lucky we were to have been stopped at Willebroeck.

By May 28 the Belgian army, under King Leopold III, had capitulated to the Germans. The first few weeks of the Occupation of Belgium were relatively uneventful. The enemy troops appeared to show a certain restraint in their dealings with the citizens. When a German soldier talked to a Belgian civilian, he seemed to go out of his way to be courteous, obviously on orders from above. Apart from the alien uniforms on the streets the city looked very much the same as it had before the war.

My father reopened the store, and the family resumed its daily chores as if nothing had happened. The Feldgendarmerie, a kind of military police assigned to check on the civilian population, had established its headquarters on our street, not far from our shop in a large apartment house at the corner of rue de la Vallée. Inevitably some of them dropped in as customers. They must surely have noticed that we were Jewish—if only by our name—but their courtesy and apparent cordiality was astonishing. Their attitude allayed our fears somewhat, which may have been their purpose. Also in our neighbourhood, on fashionable avenue Louise, the Gestapo had quietly requisitioned a brand-new eight-storey apartment building as headquarters. Despite their sinister reputation, they remained inconspicuous at first, and their presence did not disturb us.

The apparent normality and calm encouraged many people to dismiss, as mere lies, unlikely-sounding stories about cruelties in concentration camps, mass murders, and other heinous crimes attributed to the Hitler regime. The Jewish community, too, began to wonder whether rumours of persecution of Jews in Germany and elsewhere were not gross exaggerations. The German authorities certainly fostered such a false sense of security, so that many burghers believed that their best reaction to the German presence was reluctant acceptance. From such a stance to open collaboration with the enemy was, for some individuals, but a short step.

Before the summer ended, however, the Boche began to show his hand. The Kommandantur made it known through the press and posters that all able-bodied men between the ages of eighteen and fifty-five were liable to be called for work in German farms or factories, and that a certain number would be summoned as needed. The decree added that those who received the summons were to report to the authorities immediately. Anyone who failed to do so would be arrested and deported to Germany. When the bulk of the affected population ignored the orders, swift and ruthless reprisals followed. Squads of Feldgendarmes were strategically positioned at points all over Brussels, including the entrances to factories and other large establishments. As the men left work, groups of them were rounded up at random, herded into trucks, and shipped directly to Germany.

These harsh measures had the effect of hardening, rather than softening, the determination of many who had chosen to go into hiding rather than work for the enemy. Some of these banded together, eventually joining the clandestine units bent on sabotaging the invaders' aims, and thus forming a loose underground organization of patriots. This organization grew month after month into the network that became the Belgian Resistance.

The Nazis were not yet excluding men of certain races or religions from the summons when my father unexpectedly received his order. This came as a stunning blow for all of us, and especially for my father, who had just turned fifty. We agonized over his best response, for we knew that once in Germany, he would be branded as a Jew and might never come back. After consulting with friends, Father decided his best course was to fake sickness. Someone had recommended a physician to him. The doctor agreed to give him an injection to simulate the abnormal heartbeat usually associated with a weak heart. On the morning of the day he was to report to the authorities, he received the injection. After undergoing the required medical examination, he was issued a rejection slip owing to his weak heart. We celebrated his escape with great relief.

Another proclamation soon declared it a crime for anyone to listen to "foreign" radio stations other than those controlled by the Germans. This measure was intended primarily to block the BBC's broadcasts, which everyone followed faithfully. The new law also included an addendum directed at Jews, who had not been particularly singled out up to that point: they were ordered to hand in all radios in their possession within eight days, and to personally deliver their radios to one specific centre in town. Deportation was again threatened for anyone who did not co-operate.

Against my protests, my parents decided that we should comply, and they delegated my sister and me to carry our radio set to the centre, which was about three kilometres from home. Because of its bulk, we could not carry it on the trolley-cars, which were then our sole means of transportation. The radio sets of the thirties were extremely heavy and cumbersome, and ours must have weighed about thirty pounds. My sister and I, both under five feet tall, had to carry the set between us. I found the journey as humiliating as it was arduous. By the time we reached the centre, I was seething with indignation and rage against the Germans.

The scene of confusion at the centre was one I have never forgotten. There was a long line-up of people of all ages, male and female, strong and weak, thin and fat, some rich, some poor, all carrying radio sets of varying sizes, styles, and colours. The only common denominator was that all were Jews. The general mood was one of resignation and docility. A notice on the wall warned that radios were not to be deposited on the floor at any time. At the far end of the long packed hall sat a German officer behind a large table. I could not identify his rank, but I immediately detested him—perhaps because of the scar on his left cheek. He presided over the checking of the sets as they were placed on the table; he asked a few questions, scribbled something down, then ordered the sets removed to the back. Then the next person moved forward. My sister and I, each hanging onto an end of the set, inched slowly nearer to the desk. I could hear the officer addressing an old man a few places ahead of us. In a harsh guttural voice, he criticized the dilapidated state of the radio in front of him.

He did not seem to like the old man's answer, given in a subdued tone, for his features contorted. I heard him sputter insultingly in German, loud enough for all to hear, "Verdammter Jud."

The remark infuriated me so much that I could have strangled him. I had to do something, though instinct told me not to go beyond certain limits. I whispered my sudden idea to Lily. She had always been the more intelligent of the two of us, and was also much more cautious and timid. I was not surprised when she refused to co-operate. But I didn't care.

As it was our turn to approach the table, I released my end of the radio, knowing full well that Lily was not strong enough to hold the whole radio alone. The heavy set dropped on the floor with a pleasing crash, its fragile insides broken or certainly useless. The officer was enraged, and demanded to know what the hell we thought we were doing! I tried to look sheepish while replying, in German, that it was an accident. He snarled at me, "Accident be damned! You did it on purpose!" I repeated that it was really an accident, that we were very sorry but my sister and I had had to carry the heavy thing *a very long way,* and our hands were numb. Then he wanted to know why we had not deposited the apparatus on the floor. Wordlessly I pointed to the poster on the wall. When he seemed to hesitate, I was quick to reinforce my slight advantage by suggesting with an engaging smile that, after all, the German army had highly qualified technicians who would not find it hard to fix the radio. Temporarily beaten, he made a kind of grimace and dismissed us with a brusque wave of the hand.

Once we were outside, Lily, still shaking, scolded me for my recklessness and "for endangering our lives". For me, this first act of defiance represented an achievement of which I was proud.

There was a sequel to that incident. The next day my father bought a brand-new radio through a Gentile friend, as Jews were obviously no longer permitted to own radios, and he hid it in the coal cellar. Every evening the family would gather in the cellar and listen eagerly to the BBC. Often, before we could get the much-awaited news, which was broadcast in French, we had to listen first to a long string of coded messages meaningless to us, such as "Les vaches sont retournées à l'étable" or "Les bouquets sont fanés." In those early months after the Occupation, there were not many reports of Allied victories, and whatever we heard meant contact with the free outside world. That alone gave us comfort. I often grew impatient waiting for something dramatic to happen and left the stuffy cellar long before the end of the broadcast. Only my father remained glued to the set, not missing a word, later relaying the news to us. It was from the BBC that we heard the first reliable accounts of the concentration camps and the Nazi persecution of the Jews in Germany and occupied Europe. Although the dimensions of the Nazi crimes were not revealed until later in the war, those broadcasts conveyed to us the imminence of the genuine threat hanging over our heads.

2

Old Friend
in New Garb

I can no longer recall the exact date of that sunny day in the fall of 1940. My mother and I had been shopping most of the afternoon, and after walking a good deal, we decided to rest our tired feet at one of the crowded downtown cafés. In those days there were many of these dotting the semicircle formed by porte Louise, a busy intersection in Brussels. With many other shoppers, we paused here to sip tea and rest.

Several German soldiers walked in while we were there and sat down at a table not far from ours. After a few minutes I thought that one of them was staring at me. I told my mother, and she offered to change seats with me. She glanced in the direction of the soldiers and said to me in an undertone that one of them reminded her of my friend the Belgian officer; she could not remember his name. I thought she must have meant François, and out of curiosity I turned around, pretending to look towards the door. Sure enough, one did bear an uncanny resemblance to him. When I looked again, our eyes met and he nodded. His smile disclosed a gold tooth exactly where I remembered François had one. I marvelled that two such different people should be so much alike, one a Belgian officer and the other a German private.

Mother tried to reassure me. Everyone, she said, has a double somewhere, and this must have been my friend's. While we were talking, the soldier left his table and approached ours, all smiles. He addressed us politely in German, introducing himself as Franz, and offered to buy us drinks or ice cream.

I was momentarily speechless. Then I coolly thanked him, saying that we were about to leave, and suddenly realized I was answering him in German. I eyed him suspiciously and asked how he had known that I spoke the language. He laughed with the same laugh that François had had, and said he had just taken a chance, as he did not speak French himself. By now, people were beginning to stare in our direction. I was not eager to be seen fraternizing with one of the enemy. As my mother and I got up to go, I thought I noticed a brief shadow cross his face. He seemed to hesitate as if he were about to say something; then he recovered his manners, excused himself, saluted, clicked his heels, and returned to his colleagues.

Not more than a minute or two later, as we were walking on the street, we heard running footsteps behind us, and a man's voice calling out in German, "Halt! Don't go away!" A German voice ordering one to stop could not be ignored with impunity.

So we stopped, turned around, and found our smiling soldier facing us. This time he addressed my mother by name, in French: "Comment allez-vous, Madame Moszkiewiez? Vous vous rappelez sûrement de moi?" Turning to me, he said, "Bonjour, Hélène.* Je suis bien content de te revoir."

I was flabbergasted to recognize fully that the man was my friend François in German uniform. I was also disgusted when he admitted that he was really a German national who had spent some years in Belgium on a special mission. All the time I had known him, he was telling me, he had been an enemy spy. I could have slapped his face then and there.

Mother took advantage of my silence to ask him, quietly and politely, not to contact us again. She shook his hand and said goodbye, giving him no chance to say any more. He looked at me again as if he had something more to say, but then turned away.

I was overwhelmed with confusion and doubts as we walked away. In the years that I had known François, I had thought of him only as a Belgian lieutenant. His sudden reappearance out of nowhere in the disconcerting guise of a German soldier simply did not make sense. I strongly suspected that he had not told us the whole truth.

---

* Today the author prefers to spell her first name in the North American way, without accents.

Impulsively I turned and ran after him, catching up with him as he was about to turn a corner. When he saw me he paused, startled. I told him bluntly that I wanted to have a serious talk with him, alone, that same evening, if it suited him. We agreed to meet in the park at the bois de la Cambre, in a spot well away from the main traffic.

Mother was waiting for me when I ran back, and she looked very angry. I knew she would not understand how I felt, so I lied. I told her I had just wanted to give him a piece of my mind for having deceived me in the past. She scolded me, saying that it was dangerous to start a feud with a Boche, especially one like him, who knew we were Jewish and where we lived. She insisted that I learn to be more careful and hold my tongue.

That evening François—or Franz, as I shall now call him—was waiting for me. We sat down together on a nearby bench. I spoke first. I told him his story did not sound convincing. I could not understand why he had suddenly disappeared in 1939 without even saying good-bye, and I found it hard to believe he was really German, considering what he had previously told me about himself and his background. His being a mere sergeant, as he appeared to be, was an added puzzle.

He calmly confirmed that he really was German and had joined the Todt, the Wehrmacht's engineering organization, for special reasons he could not divulge to me. This answer angered me, and I told him that in that case I would leave. I said it would not be proper for me to see him again.

Unexpectedly he asked if I very much resented his being a German. I said I did not care, but my contempt must have shown. When I started to walk away, he grabbed my arm and spun me around to face him. The expression in his eyes was conciliatory and earnest, and I knew he meant no harm. He begged me not to be angry, and he swore he would tell me the truth if I would listen. We sat down again.

He truly was a loyal Belgian officer, he said, and in trying to pass for a German, he had simply tested me, to be sure he could really trust me. He said he had tried to reach me by phoning my home several times over the past few weeks, but someone else had always answered and he had not wanted to reveal himself. He had also watched for me in the street, without success. When he had seen me that afternoon, he had decided it would not be wise to tell me too much in my mother's presence. He had decided to give up, until I had asked to see him alone.

I interrupted his story. "Why this sudden renewed interest in me, though? And why now?" He explained that he and his friends in the

Resistance were looking for a girl who could speak German. Of course he thought that my being Jewish should provide extra motivation to me to work against the Nazis. I was curious to know more, so he continued.

In 1939 Franz had been assigned to intelligence work for the Belgian army because he spoke fluent German. Then, with no warning, they had ordered his transfer to a secret place near Brussels for special courses. Following this, he was sent to England for final training, and by the time he was ready for field-work, Germany had invaded Poland and war was declared. British Intelligence accordingly provided him with a German passport, identity papers, clothing, German money, and a cover story, and packed him off to Germany as a German national. His orders were to join the armed forces there until further notice, preferably the Feldgendarmerie or the Gestapo.

The German military bureaucracy, however, had chosen to post him to the Todt. When he approached me and my mother in the café, he had been in Brussels for three months, and he had requested a transfer to an intelligence unit, stressing his knowledge of French and English. After much effort he had finally contacted a Belgian Resistance group, and that is how he had learned that they were looking for a German-speaking girl. He had thought of me, as he reckoned that I could be a great help to them.

His story was plausible, but tempting though the offer was, I did not see how I could possibly become involved in Resistance work without my parents' knowledge, and I knew they would never approve of my participation. I explained this to Franz. He asked only that I think it over. He gave me his new name—Franz Boehler—and his number and the barracks where I could leave a message if I decided to contact him.

I returned home late that evening and was unable to sleep for fantasizing about myself engaged in daring cloak-and-dagger adventures. By morning Franz's story had acquired a dream-like quality when I turned it over again in my mind. I wondered how much I could believe of what he had said, and I wondered what his ulterior motives were. I finally told myself that I would be foolish to entangle myself in dangerous plots of which I knew nothing. I had been daydreaming to think otherwise, and I resolved to forget about Franz and his ideas.

3

First Steps in the Barracks

Three weeks after our meeting, Franz called on me one day when I was alone in the shop. He asked if I could spare an hour or so that evening, as he wanted to introduce me to a good friend who was eager to meet me. I hesitated, and he insisted. His friend was a member of the Resistance who needed my help. The note of urgency in his voice aroused my curiosity, but Franz would not go into details.

"Listen, Hélène, my friend's place isn't far from yours. You can be there in no time. Please do me the favour and come over. It's important. Take a taxi if you wish. I'll pay for it."

At the age of nineteen one is apt to take spontaneous chances. I agreed, and he gave me the address. That evening I slipped out of the house on the pretext of visiting a friend. I could not find a taxi, so I walked, and arrived right on time.

The place was a small, poorly furnished apartment on the first floor. Franz introduced me to Jean, a young man in his mid-twenties, medium height, with brown eyes and an open face. His handshake was firm.

When I think of Jean now, I think of the dedicated and utterly trustworthy patriot, a colleague who never let me down. I never knew him well as a private person. Even his name was a nom de guerre, and in all the years that we worked together, I never learned his real name, nor if he was single or married, whether he had a family or parents, or how he spent his spare time. I knew only that he was a master printer by trade and knowledgeable in whatever he undertook. As a member of the Resistance he naturally revealed as little as possible about himself to other members. The underground's secrecy and security were a necessity: the less each member knew about his contacts, the better his chances of survival, and theirs, if any of them were arrested and interrogated by the Gestapo.

Jean wasted no time in formalities: "Franz tells me you are fluent in German, and I can see for myself that you are attractive enough, and look younger than your age. We need a girl just like you to help us in our fight against the Boches." When I asked what kind of help would be expected of me, he said he could tell me nothing until he could be sure that I was ready and willing to work for the Resistance—which, in this case, meant working for London as well. Most of the numerous underground groups in the Belgian Resistance were aided and instructed by British Intelligence.

I said that I lived with my parents, who were very strict, and that my freedom of movement was therefore somewhat limited. I also wanted to know what risks were involved.

Jean warned me that my parents were to know nothing about my work or my connection with the Resistance. He did not think my own work would be very dangerous, but he wanted me to understand that there would always be some risk in whatever we did.

I must have looked hesitant because Franz intervened. He said that London had ordered him to get himself transferred to a more sensitive job, like the Feldgendarmerie or the Gestapo, or to desert the Todt and join one of the maquis, groups like Jean's that operated from camps hidden in the countryside. With a wistful look, he added that with his background, training, and knowledge of languages, he could be of much greater use to the Resistance, and our common cause, and that my help would be invaluable to him.

I vacillated and asked to think it over. Jean nodded and gave me his telephone number to call once I had decided. And he warned me that whatever I decided, nothing of our meeting could be repeated to anyone, parents or friends. I promised silence.

My mind was in turmoil for the next few days. I knew that working with the Resistance could eventually destroy not only me, but my parents as well. And I had to reckon with Lily. She knew me very well, and I foresaw difficulties in keeping Resistance activities secret from her. She was always trying to keep me out of trouble, real or imagined.

In the meantime grim news continued to trickle in from the BBC, particularly for the Jews. We heard growing confirmation of their systematic and ruthless persecution in Germany, Poland, and elsewhere in Europe, about yellow stars, mass arrests, families torn apart, and hundreds of people sent to concentration camps.

In Belgium, Jews were feeling more and more insecure. My parents were increasingly anxious as sales at the store had dropped considerably over the months. In an effort to improve business, Father had hired an assistant tailor who needed work, a hunchback who did odd tailoring jobs for our customers. Émile was a quiet, good-natured fellow who squatted in one corner of the store all day, plying his trade, and who did not mind getting up to help with the sales. My own presence behind the counter gradually became superfluous, and I had plenty of time to think and brood about myself and the future.

As a child I had dreamed of becoming a dancer, and I had identified with Isadora Duncan. My parents, however, did not think such dreams sufficient reason to pay for costly dancing lessons they could ill afford. Later I dreamed of being a coloratura, for I had a good soprano voice. I even managed to obtain an audition and a few lessons from Joseph Schmidt, the world-renowned tenor, who was living in Brussels at the time. Since he too was a Jew, he had refused to accept fees for my lessons; but unfortunately he left for Switzerland soon after my studies began, and he died there during the war. He was a wonderful teacher and his departure affected me deeply. It also meant an end to any operatic ambitions.

My school years had been an academic disaster, for I had seen school as a battleground. In Belgium in those days boys and girls were segregated into separate schools. All our teachers, as well as the principal, were women. My favourite subjects were diction, song, and gymnastics—in which I excelled—subjects scorned by most of my teachers. They often compared me with my sister, who had been a brilliant student at the same school before me and had won all kinds of prizes. Since I showed little interest in the other subjects, I was considered one of the dunces. Out of resentment I gave my teachers a hard time. Though I was slender and the shortest in my class, I became the leader of a gang at recess time and carried a heavy ruler, which I used as a weapon against anyone who dared to antagonize me. Above all else I hated injustice, and I reacted fiercely when anyone offended my rigid sense of fairness or insulted my race. My followers were mostly tall, fat, placid, and timid girls in need of leadership. I was feared, and therefore respected. My mother used to call me a defender of lost causes and stray dogs. (I often brought home some lost pooch.)

Mlle Thielemans, our diction teacher, a short, fat, and ugly spinster of indeterminate age, was rumoured to wear a wig. Women in the 1930s rarely wore wigs, except on the stage, so this singularity made Mlle T., as we used to call her, the subject of wild conjectures and mockeries when she was out of earshot.

One day she called me to stand in front of the class beside her to recite a poem, which was considered a particular honour. In the middle of my recitation, a lout of a girl named Anna, who was also Jewish though no friend of mine, interrupted my performance with loud giggles. Mlle T. sternly reprimanded her as she deserved, and ordered her out of the room. Then she called Anna "a dirty kike" in front of the whole class.

This kind of insult I could not, and still cannot, ignore, no matter to whom directed. In one impulsive move, I snatched the wig off her head and flung it across the room. Then I hurried to pick it up and ran straight to the washroom, where I dipped it in a toilet bowl before returning to the classroom. Wordlessly I handed the sodden mess to the bald teacher. During that short episode the class had remained absolutely silent.

Mlle Thielemans immediately hauled me before the principal, where I was asked to explain my behaviour.

"In insulting Anna, Mlle Thielemans insulted me as well. I am Jewish. I reacted automatically." For my reaction I could have been expelled, but instead I was severely reprimanded and sent back to class. Before that incident Mlle T. had not known that I was Jewish. The following week Mlle T. appeared in class wearing a brand-new wig. Curiously enough, she never held a grudge against me, and I remained her best and favourite student.

Such reminiscences of my schooldays did little to help me in my decision at age nineteen. My work at home and in the shop had become boring to me, and I fretted, restless for greater freedom. I resented the oppressive presence of the Nazis that made a happier teen-aged existence impossible. Their ever-growing persecution of Jews fed my frustrations and fuelled my enmity. Not only would I be better able to retaliate against the Nazis if I were to join the Resistance, but I would partially escape the monotony of my home life. I decided to accept Jean's offer.

At our next meeting Franz was present, but Jean did all the talking. He asked if I was absolutely sure of my decision, because once I enrolled in the underground, there could be no turning back. I had heard rumours of traitors, and even defectors, who had been summarily executed by the maquis. But my mind was made up. I replied that if I were caught by the Boches, at least it would be not because I was Jewish but because I had been fighting the enemy. And before I was killed, I would make damned sure to take a few of the "salauds" with me.

My response seemed to please Jean. He immediately began to brief me on my first mission, which he said was a simple one. I was to sell German newspapers and magazines to German soldiers stationed around the city, to familiarize myself with the barracks. I was to report whatever I heard or observed to him directly. I would be told where to pick up German publications; how I actually accomplished the assignment was left to me. He promised that training for other missions would come later.

My task was not as easy as it originally appeared to be. My first problem lay in overcoming my father's objections. He said he could understand that I wanted to earn some extra money and that every little bit helped in these hard times. But why had I chosen to deal in German publications? What was wrong with the Belgian ones, French or Flemish? I told him that there was little money to be made selling them, whereas I could make a good profit selling German papers and magazines. After days of arguments, I finally wore down both parents' resistance.

Next I had to gain admittance to the barracks. The first one I approached was called Petits-Carmes, after the street of that name. They must have been some of the oldest barracks in Brussels. They looked dilapidated even then and have probably been torn down since. With my bundle of papers firmly tied down on the back of my bicycle, I went straight to the soldier on guard by the sentry-box. I asked in German if I could be allowed to peddle papers inside.

The soldier was a man of about forty who answered me with kind concern, as if he believed that I had innocently strayed onto forbidden ground. "Don't you know, my child, that civilians are not allowed in the barracks?"

I asked if he would mind if I spoke to the commanding officer; I felt sure he would give me permission. He hesitated, and then, shrugging his shoulders, pointed to a door a few feet inside the passage, which he said was the CO's office.

A crisp "Herein!" answered my knock at the door. The colonel looked most surprised to find me standing in front of him, and he asked what I wanted. I told him, slightly embroidering my request with a hard-luck story. At this he looked even more taken aback. He shook his head. He said it would not be proper to let a young girl loose amongst all those hungry soldiers—if I knew what he meant.

I assured him I was only trying to make a living and was sure that his soldiers would not dare to molest a girl of my age.

Then, as if just making a discovery, he asked me where I had learned German. At school? I answered that my mother was German. This interested him, and he wanted to know my name.

The first name that came to mind was Rubens, so I told him I was Hella Rubens, and that my father was Belgian. He repeated the name thoughtfully and asked, with a chuckle, whether by any chance I would be a descendant of the famous painter.

I shook my head and said, "I don't know, but I guess I should be rich if I were." He nodded, smiling, and rang a bell. An officer, perhaps a major, entered and saluted sharply. The colonel informed him that I was half German and wanted permission to sell newspapers and magazines to the other ranks. As an afterthought, he added that it was a patriotic thing to do, did the major not agree? The major endorsed the idea enthusiastically, adding that it would be good for the general morale of the troops. The colonel remained non-committal and told the major he would leave it to him, if he thought it would be all right. The major asked me to bring two passport photographs to him the next morning, and he promised to issue a pass in my name.

The next day I received my permit for Hella Rubens. To my amazement I was not asked for identity papers or even my address. Clearly not all the Wehrmacht officers, particularly those of the older generation, were as security-conscious as I had expected.

I was now free to come and go with my Ausweis in hand, and I soon made myself a familiar figure in the barracks, where I appeared almost every day. I was especially popular with the other ranks, who not only regularly bought my papers but plied me with pocketfuls of chocolate, cookies, and even bread and fresh butter. All these items were in scarce supply to civilians and were therefore worth their weight in gold. Accounting for these daily bounties to my parents without disclosing their origin taxed my imagination. I accordingly concocted a plausible story about black-market transactions, which would actually have been impossible on my meagre earnings.

I was surprised to find how little enthusiasm some of the older soldiers showed for soldiering. I remember one in particular, a nondescript private of about forty, evidently of peasant background. He called me one day to buy a newspaper; as soon as he had paid me, he spread the paper on his bunk and carefully wrapped his boots in it. Surprised, I asked if he wasn't going to at least read it first. He mumbled something about not caring to read all that crap; then, bending over to me, his face almost touching mine, he whispered, "All I want, child, is to get back to my family and farm."

I realized then that not every German soldier was happy to lay down his life for the greater glory of the Führer and the Vaterland. Franz translated this attitude as "low morale in the army". He also referred to the constant turn-over of barracks personnel I reported to him as an indication of troop movement. To me such pickings seemed insignificant, but neither Franz nor Jean agreed with me. On the contrary, they said, I was doing very well, and they suggested that I might approach the more important Etterbeek barracks, which were next to a military airfield and ammunition dump.

There I repeated my ploy with the sentry on guard, fortified by my Ausweis from the Petits-Carmes barracks. To my disappointment, he listened to me very politely, but firmly refused to let me enter. A passing officer also listened sympathetically to my request, thought my motives laudable, but insisted that orders were very strict. No civilians were allowed admittance. He kindly suggested I set up shop on the curb outside. He even went out of his way to provide me with a trestle-table on which to display my wares. Thus I was in business again, but essentially out in the cold, as it were.

In Brussels the month of March is more often an extension of winter than a forerunner of spring. The days were rainy, chilly, and generally miserable. Unlike those at the Petits-Carmes, faces here did not change very much, and I found very little worth reporting from my stall. When I complained to Franz that I was wasting my time there, he lectured me on espionage, explaining that the smallest bit of information, however trivial it might seem to me, would find its place in the giant jigsaw puzzle that the British War Office was constantly piecing together to halt the enemy's advance. The idea did not impress me. Franz urged me to be patient, promising that soon they would find something more exciting for me to do. So I went back to my stall and my papers, though not very happily.

When I arrived at the stall a few days later, there was unusual activity at the barracks. Officers were bustling to and fro and barking orders to the men, who were kept moving on the double. I hailed one passing soldier and asked him what all the commotion was about. He replied that everyone was preparing for inspection by some VIP general that afternoon.

He was right. Later in the day, an array of bemedalled generals and assorted high-ranking officers grandly emerged from their respective limousines only a few yards from my stall. A corresponding group of officers and men emerged from the barracks to meet them, and froze at attention. As the visitors passed my stand, a large pudgy general with a porcine face stopped and glanced at my display of magazines, nodding his weighty approval. He turned to his companions and made some comments, of which I could only hear "Good for the morale of the troops." He smiled at me, shook my hand briefly, and gave me a tap on the cheek with his hairy paw, saying something like "Good work." Moments later the entourage had disappeared into the compound. One of the sentries came over to congratulate me warmly on the great honour to have been singled out by Herr Marschall Göring himself. I pretended to be proud and even delighted, though all I really felt was contempt and disgust. As soon as I had a chance, however, I went and thoroughly washed my hands.

Jean told me that a recent message from London had announced imminent air raids on some of the Brussels barracks. He advised me to be watchful and take shelter on the first alert. A week later I awoke at about half past six, aroused by the wailing of sirens that signalled an approaching raid. I heard the distant explosions but had no idea where the bombs had fallen. At nine o'clock, when I cycled to the site where I usually erected my stall, I found a scene of destruction and pandemonium. Smoke was rising everywhere from inside the compound, where entire buildings were on fire and others had collapsed. Soldiers hurried clumsily through the rubble, removing casualties who were then borne away in army trucks. Barriers had been erected on the street, forcing the public, as well as all vehicles, to make a lengthy detour.

My first reaction was tremendous relief that the raid had happened when it did, sparing me from probable injury or worse. I also felt keen satisfaction at this set-back for the enemy. I learned some time later that the Allied bombers had missed their primary target, the ammunition dump, and I regretted this. In any case the air raid ended my mission at the barracks, as the danger it now involved was not justified by the scant information I could obtain.

Franz advised me to relax and await further orders, hinting that he had something important in store for me. It was not long afterwards that I prepared for my second mission.

4

Vamping Around the Abbey

The Abbaye de la Cambre in Brussels, which dates from the Middle
Ages, occupies a large parcel of land east of avenue Louise, not far
from the bois de la Cambre, a large wooded park to the south. It is
surrounded by gardens and parkland that were once the monks' exclusive grounds but have been open to the public since the last century.
In my time, the abbey's immediate neighbourhood was the preserve of
the aristocratic upper class; its residents lived in stately mansions, or
hôtels privés.

Long before the war, probably as far back as the turn of the century, part of the abbey proper had been converted into headquarters
for the Belgian army's cartography section. The German army of
occupation took possession of the venerable building and continued to
use it for its own cartography unit. In the meantime the park remained open to the public. It was still a peaceful place, only ten
minutes' walk from my home, and I often spent an idle hour there.

Franz and Jean had a "job" in mind for me at the abbey. At our
next meeting, soon after the air raid, Franz summarized his plan: I
was to infiltrate the cartography unit in the same way that I had
infiltrated the barracks, by selling German publications to the staff
there. Jean expressed his doubts about the potential success of the
project, for the premises were top secret, heavily guarded, and strongly

protected by a high fence of barbed wire. He considered it most unlikely that I would be granted admittance.

Not only did I share Jean's misgivings, but I was not overly pleased by the prospect of peddling more papers. Franz pointed out that the job was far more interesting than I thought; it could give me access to sensitive information, and even enable me to get hold of some maps— "if I played my cards right." With a wry smile he added that I would have to befriend some of the officers there, become very close to them, and gain their confidence.

I understood him, though I was not ready to do this. I knew I could not overcome my ingrained fears of possible consequences, and the mere thought of going to bed with an enemy soldier disgusted me. I obviously lacked what it took to make a Mata Hari. I told Franz that there were limits to my dedication. Mission or no mission, I would not go to bed with a German officer. He merely urged me to give the job a try, adding that, after all, the manner in which I obtained results was no concern of his.

The following Monday I piled my bundle of newspapers and magazines on my bicycle and pedalled off to the abbey. I was surprised to find a full-fledged lieutenant on sentry duty at the entrance rather than the usual corporal or private. I showed him my pass, the one issued by the Petits-Carmes barracks, in a matter-of-fact and friendly way. He dismissed me shortly.

I assumed the role of what I considered my "deutsches Mädchen": "My, but you *are* in a bad mood, Herr Leutnant. Anything the matter? Perhaps you had a fight with your girlfriend, ja?" He replied that no civilian was allowed on the premises. I was sorry to hear this, I said, as I was only trying to make an honest living, and I had an Ausweis as he could see, and so on. My purpose was not so much personal persuasion, for I knew he had no authority, but to play for time, hoping for the chance to appeal for a second opinion.

In fact, another officer of an obviously higher rank did emerge from the building, and he asked to know what was going on. He listened to me and smirked, looking me over in such a way that I was apprehensive when he invited me to follow him inside. We passed along a narrow hall and into a large office, where he snapped to attention before another officer sitting behind a desk covered with papers. He was an older man with kindly features whom I took to be the CO. After listening to a very brief report on the reason for my presence, the CO dismissed my guide, offered me a seat, and asked me to explain myself again. I did so and handed him my pass. He studied it while he interrogated me.

"Aren't you selling your papers at the barracks any more, my child?" I decided that it was a good sign that he had adopted a fatherly attitude.

"Not any more, Herr Oberst. My parents say it is too dangerous because of the bombings."

"How is it that you speak such good German?"

"My mother is German, but my father is Belgian."

"And why don't you sell French papers?"

"There is very little profit in them. I make much more money selling German ones."

"I see." Then he suddenly asked, "Who do you think is going to win the war?"

"But what a question, Herr Oberst! The German armies are advancing on all fronts and winning. Can there be any doubt? I think the war will soon be over."

"And whom do you like better, the Belgians or the Germans?"

"To be quite frank, as long as people behave decently, they are all the same to me."

He seemed to approve of my answer, for he nodded. He thought for a while, then said, "I am going to make an exception for you. I will allow you to come in and sell your papers. But I must warn you that, on occasions, you may be searched by the sentry. Also, you are to knock on each door and enter only when you are invited to. If there is no answer you will not enter. Is that understood?"

"Yes, I understand, Herr Oberst, and thank you very much." I looked as humble as I could. He wrote something on my pass, signed it, stamped it, and handed it to me with a smile. "Good luck."

I was jubilant with my success. Jean and Franz were also delighted and they congratulated me warmly.

Before long I had become a familiar presence at Cartography. Inevitably several of the officers made passes at me. One of them, a young lieutenant named Hugo Stahler, was particularly persistent. He was red-headed, tall and angular, with a nose sticking out of his face like a beak, eagle-fashion. He was as vain as a peacock and considered himself irresistible to women. Grimly I forced myself to be amiable to him, and finally I accepted a date in the hope of gathering any useful information.

My parents gave me full freedom to go out in the evenings as long as I was home by eleven. They knew I had numerous friends of both sexes, and they trusted me, only very occasionally asking where I had been and what I had done. The only problem I could see in going out with a German officer was keeping out of sight of friends and acquaintances. I accordingly chose as meeting-places remote cafés and small bistros where my chances of meeting anyone I knew were minimal.

I went out with Hugo a couple of times, although I found him extremely boring, and I learned little of interest. He had been some sort of draughtsman for a plumbing and heating concern before the war, and he repeated over and over again how proud he was to fight for the Vaterland, and how lucky "we" were to have such a wonderful Führer as Adolf Hitler. He was also set on going to bed with me and made no secret of it. He had evidently thought I would co-operate very cheerfully. On our second evening out, he wanted to take me to his room, but I put him off with some excuse.

When I did not see him at Cartography for a couple of weeks, I thought he had been transferred, and I felt relieved, especially as my spying on him had been fruitless. But he came back, as interested in me as before.

This time he invited me for dinner. Although I doubted that I would get anything out of him, I felt it might not be wise to refuse him too suddenly. I accepted the invitation on the condition that he behave. He seemed to be in high spirits during our dinner at a small restaurant. Half-way through the meal I noticed an extra red stripe on his uniform collar, which I did not remember having seen before. I pointed this out and innocently asked what it meant. He proudly announced that he had been promoted. I congratulated him warmly, adding that I knew he would go far. He could not resist bragging. He confided that he would soon be transferred to a better post, in France. He called me his "Schätzchen"—his little treasure—and tried once more to persuade me to come to his room. I said maybe next time, hoping he would be gone by then.

When I saw Franz later that week, I told him that Hugo did not seem to know very much. As an afterthought I mentioned that he had been promoted. Franz warned me that the extra red stripe on Hugo's uniform was a badge of the Abwehr, German military intelligence, and that I should now avoid the man, as he should be considered dangerous. In any case he was not likely to give out any information of value.

Luckily for me, Hugo Stahler left Cartography very soon after our talk, which was a great relief. We were, however, to meet again some time later, with dramatic consequences.

Meanwhile another officer, Hauptmann Alfred Hermann, had also been watching me with growing interest. He was a very industrious character, much committed to his mapwork. A captain of about forty, he had a kind face and intelligent eyes. His uniform belied the civilian professional. Whenever he saw me, he complimented me with flattering old-fashioned gallantry, though he had not yet openly asked me for a date. He seemed to me to be a more likely source of information than Hugo had ever been; he was evidently very timid with women, so I decided that I would have to take the initiative.

Every officer took guard duty in turn. My opportunity came one day when Hermann was alone on guard. I stopped for a chat and casually asked if he knew the picturesque nooks and corners of Brussels, apart from the Grand'Place. He said he did not, then brightened and suggested that I be his guide. We began taking walks together, and I steered our steps as far as possible from my home grounds. Sometimes we visited wayside cafés or quaint little restaurants, hidden from the mainstream of traffic. He spared no expense when we went out for drinks or for dinner, though he himself was markedly abstemious. Stahler had quaffed beer at every opportunity whereas Hermann seldom drank more than one glass of wine or sherry at a sitting. From our conversations I learned that he was a married man with no children, a professional cartographer in civilian life, and that he did not care for politics. I gathered that he did not entirely approve of the Nazi creed, and especially of their ferocious persecution of the Jews. Overall he gave me the impression of a peace-loving burgher who must have been bewildered by Hitler's Reich and his popularity.

On one occasion he admitted that being able to talk to a girl in his own language meant a lot to him, as he did not speak French and was rather shy. He knew that I lived with my parents, but when he wanted to know my address, I gave him a false one in a distant suburb for fear that he might want to ferret out my real background and religion. For added security I warned him that my parents must not know about our meetings, as they would strongly object to my seeing a married man. He often gave me foodstuffs like bread, butter, meat, and other delicacies, all of which were scarce for the civilian population; these he said he scrounged from the officers' mess.

Alfred Hermann was a man of habit. He finished work at the office around four o'clock and left with a briefcase under his arm. Once when I asked him why he carried the case everywhere, he told me that it contained documents and maps on which he had to work at home, and that they were safer with him than at the office. When we went out together in the afternoon, he would go first to his apartment—which was only a few minutes away from the abbey—to carefully lock up the case.

When I had been going out with him for several weeks, I reported to Franz that I was getting nowhere with this officer, who, though friendly enough, shut up as soon as I tried to steer the conversation to his work or even to general news of the war. The only time he had mentioned any documents was when I had asked him about his brief-case. I did not see any reason to continue seeing him.

Franz did not agree. He considered Alfred's concern for his brief-case a sign that he handled sensitive material. I had to be friendlier, he told me, get to know the man better, become more intimate. This would weaken his defences and prompt him to talk more freely; eventually I might well be able to glean some really useful information. I consented, though not without some reservations.

My task was more complicated than it first appeared to be. I always had to ensure that I was not seen in the company of a German officer by an acquaintance; and I worried that my parents would hear about my "dates" and misinterpret my behaviour.

Once Hermann even offered me the present of three pairs of silk stockings—in those days absolutely unobtainable by civilians and worth a small fortune. Reluctantly I had to refuse them as I would have been hard put to account for them to my parents and friends. Some girls during those years prostituted themselves with the occupying soldiers for a pair of silk stockings, and this was common knowledge.

Whatever his ulterior motives, and they were probably no different from Hugo's, I must confess that I liked him as a person. He was a gentleman at heart, well behaved, attentive, and kind-hearted to a fault. Perhaps because Alfred was some twenty years my senior, I felt safe with him and somehow protected, feelings I had never enjoyed in my relations with younger men. This fact did not make my duties as a spy any easier for me.

I was continuing to see Alfred once a week, sometimes twice, when my parents heard about him from my sister. She had learned from a friend that someone had seen me with him in a café. Lily accordingly reported to my mother that I was "running around with German officers".

The confrontation was awkward. My parents said they had known that my selling papers to Germans would come to no good, and that they had been against it from the beginning. My father threatened to confine me at home if I did not stop "all this nonsense". My mother reminded me that I had a steady boy-friend and that I was being most unfair to him. Actually I had never really thought of my friend Albert as a steady boy-friend, and certainly not as a fiancé; but my mother liked Albert, who also happened to be a distant relative of hers, and she hoped that I would marry him one day.

Irked by the accusations, I naturally denied everything. Finally, I promised to give up selling the papers. I informed Franz of my difficulties, and he insisted that I maintain my friendship with Alfred. He was sure that I would eventually unearth a good deal of information from him.

By the time I saw Alfred again, I had concocted a story for him. I confessed reluctantly that I had a steady boy-friend whom my parents considered a future son-in-law. The boy-friend had seen us together and told my parents. I was now forbidden to sell my newspapers, and I stressed to him that we could not be seen together in public places.

He seemed deeply affected by the news. I reminded him that, being a married man, he should not take the news too seriously. He considered carefully and at last suggested that we meet in his apartment if and when I wished. This was precisely what Franz would have planned, and I agreed. I trusted him, and I did not have the slightest intention of having an affair with him.

What he called his apartment was no more than a large room in a building specially requisitioned for the use of officers. The room was as bare as an office, its furnishings consisting of only a large table, a few chairs, and a steel locker. A pair of heavy drapes divided the room into an informal sitting room and sleeping area, or bedroom.

Inevitably, when I had visited his lodgings several times for drinks, he suggested that we have dinner there and spend an evening together. I accepted the invitation with no qualms, in the hope that he might open up during the course of the evening and reveal something about his work at the abbey.

When I arrived that evening around eight o'clock, his table was already laden with an assortment of dishes direct from the officers' mess. In the midst of it all stood a bottle of white wine and two glasses. All I remember specifically now of that meal with Alfred is roast pork, red cabbage, and potatoes.

Without much preamble we sat down to eat. I was hungry and ate with gusto while I kept up the conversation. Half-way through dinner

I noticed with some unease that Alfred was drinking considerably more than usual. In fact, he had easily finished the whole of one bottle before I had touched my second glass. I noticed, too, that he did not hold his liquor well. His face became gradually flushed and his manner bolder. He took my hand and warmly pressed his lips to it, and then started to caress and kiss my bare arm. I gently removed his hand and told him to stop and to behave himself, but he did not seem to hear me.

His attention shifted to the empty bottle, and he rose to open the locker. I watched with growing interest as he fumbled with a chain around his neck for the key. A few moments later he triumphantly produced a stoneware bottle of Steinhäger, or schnapps. The locker door was left open, and I recognized the black briefcase on the lower shelf.

He offered me the schnapps, which I declined with a smile and a shake of my head, indicating my still half-full glass. Alfred shrugged and smoothly upended the bottle himself, all the while fixing me with glinting blue eyes and talking about the depth of his feelings for me. He also shifted his chair to a position beside mine and slipped his arm around my shoulders. When he eventually mustered the bravado to try to kiss me on the lips, I pushed him firmly away, reminding him that he was married.

I had certainly realized much earlier that he intended to seduce me and I had no intention of co-operating. I now gently helped him refill his glass as he emptied it and hoped that he would drink himself into a stupor before long, and even forget my presence. I was not particularly alarmed: he was not a naturally violent man. I mentioned once or twice that I should be leaving, as it was late, but he did not seem to hear me. Finally, after one final attempt to kiss me, he unsteadily rose and staggered towards his bedroom, calling me slurringly to join him. He grandly fumbled with the drapes, swung stumbling with them several feet, and crumpled ignobly to the floor. Concerned that he might have hurt himself, I helped him stand again and slowly guided him to bed, where he collapsed for good. I arranged him comfortably there and straightened the pillow under his head. He snored thickly in response.

I left him to run immediately to the locker. The briefcase itself was not locked. I hurriedly removed the maps, slid them under my dress, and rushed to the door, terrified that I would meet another officer along the way. I knew that it was past midnight, well past my parents' curfew time. Breathless, I ran all the way home, meeting no one, and hoping that my parents would be sound asleep. To my good fortune the house was absolutely still. I crept to my room, slid the maps under the carpet, and fell into bed myself, exhausted.

The next day I met Franz in the late afternoon and proudly presented the stolen maps to him. He scanned them briefly, thanked me, and, departing from his usual reserve, praised me for being such a fast worker. He thought the maps were not complete, but he would send them on to London anyway. He advised me now to avoid Hermann altogether.

I argued with that instruction. Avoiding Alfred would only reinforce his suspicions of me as the thief. I insisted that it would be wiser for me to actually visit him that evening. Franz thought the risk too great but he did not argue much; he merely said it was my life, not his. I told him not to worry.

That evening, when I knew Alfred would be home, I knocked on his door. At the sight of me he stood transfixed at the door, then he admitted me without a word and without his usual smile. He did not invite me to sit down. I said that I had just come by to see how he felt after the previous night's drinking bout. I excused myself for having left, but it had been very late, and I had had to hurry home.

He was silent for a few seconds. Then with barely controlled anger, he demanded to know when I had arrived home. Where did I live? And why had I stolen his maps? What had I done with them?

I answered each question as if I firmly believed I told the truth: it had taken me over an hour to get home; why did he need my address all of a sudden? He knew that my parents would object to our liaison. As for his maps, I had not the slightest idea what he was talking about. I added that he did not seem to be his usual self, but that it must have been the result of the previous night's excesses.

He waved an impatient hand and repeated determinedly that I had stolen the maps because I had seen his locker left open. Why had I done this: as a practical joke, perhaps? Or a dirty trick? Whatever the reason, I was to please return them to him right away.

I feigned utter amazement. What did he think I could possibly do with his maps, and why was he accusing me? He had probably left them at the office. He retorted that he had already checked there.

I seized the opportunity that his obvious uncertainty offered me. Anyone, I said, could have stolen papers from him if the locker had been open all night. Despite my arguments, he did not believe me; he now threatened me: "Listen, you little cheat, if you do not return those maps to me, I'll have you arrested. Not only that, but I'll have your place searched from top to bottom, and torn apart if necessary."

I reckoned that he could not legally prove any of his accusations, so I held to my story. I assured him that he had made a mistake. He would be wasting his time to have my home searched, since he could not find what I didn't have. As a final argument I said that if I had really stolen those documents "or whatever", I would certainly not have been foolish enough to come back to see him.

He said he had already thought of that, but was sure I had returned to his place to see what had happened, and whether he had been arrested.

In a hurt tone of voice, I retorted that after going out with me for all this time, he ought to know me better.

With a slightly wistful look he muttered, "Yes, I thought I knew you. But I didn't. I was a fool. I believed you had some feelings for me, while all the time you were only scheming to use me. Now I see it. You are a good actress, I must grant you that." His features hardened, and he asked me curtly again whether or not I intended to return the maps. He warned that this was my last chance. I shrugged. I could not return what I did not have.

He seemed lost in thought for a moment; then, staring over my head, he spoke with calm finality, as if pronouncing a verdict: "I am going to have you arrested. Right now. You leave me no choice. If I don't, they will arrest me."

For the first time my confidence was really shaken, and I shuddered at the implications—torture by the Gestapo, shipment to a concentration camp, and an ugly death. At difficult moments some instinct, like an inner voice, has always prompted me to do or say whatever was immediately necessary. Perhaps it is merely presence of mind, or even inspiration. Whatever it is, I know that without it, and without some luck, I would not be alive today.

Looking at him directly I said, "If that is your decision, then let me tell you something. As soon as you have me arrested, the Gestapo will learn that you have been consorting with a Jewess. *I* am Jewish. And that is not all. I will tell them that you are the one who stole the maps *for* me, knowing full well that they were intended for the enemy. You must realize what this would mean for you, Alfred. Not only dishonour but a choice of tortures by the Gestapo or, if you are lucky, the firing squad. Believe me, I will drag you all the way down with me. And I mean every word."

He looked horrified: "You, a Jewess? My God! But that is impossible! I would have known!"

That infuriated me. "You see? You are no better than your rotten friends, the dirty Boches, as we call them. For you, the Jew is an animal that must be destroyed because you are the pure and superior race, aren't you? But the truth is that this animal, the Jew, is far more intelligent than your superior race, and that is what you and your friends cannot stand. Go ahead, have me arrested. What are you waiting for? Don't tell me you're scared?" He was staring at me, speechless and frozen.

By that point I was worked up to a feverish pitch: "All those big gas ovens being built in Germany; what do you think they are being built for? Baking your cakes? Or cooking your dinners? No! They are meant to burn us, the Jews! Well, I can tell you, the world is not going to stand quietly by and let you murderers get away with it! Never! You will never, *never* win this war!"

Chalk white, he had slumped into a chair as I spoke. He must have felt utterly trapped. He finally rose and began to pace the room automatically, his head bowed in thought.

When he finally spoke, his voice was weary. He wondered aloud why he had not guessed all along that there must have been some ulterior motive for a girl like me to flirt with a man twice her age. He had been a fool to think I might have been interested in him as a man, when my aim had been only to get hold of his maps. At least, he said, the maps I had stolen lacked the vital information that he had been about to add that night. I would surely be the laughing-stock of my superiors, whoever they were.

"I don't pretend to be a master spy or a Mata Hari. But I want you to know that I will not be just picked up and sent to a concentration camp because I am Jewish. If your friends catch me, it will have to be for a better reason than that. And, believe me, I will give a good account of myself. If I burn, I swear some of you will burn with me."

My second outburst silenced him again. After a moment I spoke more kindly. "Alfred, be smart. Forget you ever met me. Don't try to find me, because if I am caught, it will also be the end of you. Also, though you may not believe me, I am very sorry that this had to happen. I really have nothing personal against you. Believe it or not, I hold you in great esteem, for you have always been very kind to me. I really liked you because you are different from the others, because you are a better man. That's all I have to say."

Before he could recover, I said, "Good luck," and was gone. I ran home as fast as I could, fearing that he might change his mind and follow me. But he didn't.

When I finally turned the corner of my own street, panting frantically, I could distinguish the figure of a man standing near our house. I was instantly terrified that he might be someone waiting to arrest me. I turned and started to run, when, to my immense relief, he shouted, "Hélène! It's me, Jean! Why are you running away?"

As we strolled down the street together, he told me why he needed to see me so urgently. The Resistance was tracking an extremely dangerous man, a German officer who specialized in catching agents, particularly British ones. London wanted him eliminated, but the Resistance had to be sure it was on to the right man. This is where I came in, he said. He had a snapshot of the suspected officer, and when he had first seen it, he had remembered the officer I had once befriended at the abbey. He remembered my unflattering description to him of the officer's facial features, and he wanted me to have a look at it.

We stepped into a doorway where he showed me the picture by the light of his flashlight. I immediately recognized Hugo Stahler's beaklike nose and close-set eyes. Since I had felt sure he had been transferred to France by that time, his sudden reappearance astonished me. Jean surprised me even further by saying that the snapshot had been taken by a Resistance agent only a few days before, in Brussels, at place Sainte-Croix. My "friend in France" could be found on almost any day at the Café Sainte-Croix, which he seemed to be using as a base for his assignments. I remembered his Abwehr badge and mentioned it to Jean, but he already knew about it.

Then I summarized my recent confrontation with Alfred Hermann to Jean, telling him how, with incredible luck, I had escaped. He listened without commenting. He already knew about the maps from Franz. Suddenly I was very tired and only wanted to go home to sleep. I bid Jean good night.

He asked me to listen to him for a few more minutes; what he had to tell me concerned Hugo Stahler and could not wait. Since I was the only one who knew him personally, the Resistance needed me to help. Jean wanted me to join him at the Café Sainte-Croix the next evening, around eight-thirty. During the hours before that time I had to be at home, for he would phone me to confirm arrangements. He refused to give me any more details. I said that I was finding it difficult to continue such assignments without my parents' knowledge, and that I had to invent new excuses every time. All the sympathy I got from him was a shrug and a hug, and the trite remark "À la guerre comme à la guerre" (roughly, one must take things as they come). With that remark he left me standing in the street, bewildered.

Jean, of course, was far more experienced in Resistance work and had been further steeled by his training with the underground, whereas I was a novice just beginning to understand the implications of my own commitment. I did not feel very sure just then that I could actually perform the tasks assigned to me. I hoped so.

5

Countering a Counter-spy

It was nearly nine that night when Jean called. Hugo was at the Café Sainte-Croix with two other officers; I was to join Jean as soon as possible, before ten o'clock if I could make it. He would be sitting at a table by himself.

I was not sure my father would let me go out at that hour; he had been suspicious of my activities ever since our earlier confrontation over Alfred Hermann. I promised to try my best; if he did not see me by ten o'clock, he was to assume that I could not make it. His last words were simply, "Do your utmost. I count on you." I racked my brains for a valid excuse. Then I remembered Albert, my would-be fiancé, whom I had not seen for some time and who was a most welcome guest in my parents' home. With him as an escort, I could easily slip out. I also knew that I could count on him to co-operate with few questions.

We had known each other since childhood. He was a very distant cousin as well as a friend of the family, and he formed part of my circle of friends. He was a year younger than me, a good-looking and clean-cut young man, and over six feet tall. The top of my head did not quite reach his shoulders. I had always treated him as a pal, and so was very surprised when he had asked me earlier that year to be his girl-friend. He swore that he felt very strongly about me, and he hoped I would eventually reciprocate his feelings. As I did not wish to hurt him, I had agreed to go out with him, but not on a steady basis. I told him that I did not feel ready for any firm commitments. Our discrepancies in height and age had bothered me at first when I was out with him, though in time I grew accustomed to them. My mother had been much encouraged by this development and hinted broadly that he would make a good husband.

I called him and was fortunate enough to find him at home. I asked him to come over right away and ask me out for the evening, but not to mention to my parents that this was my idea. He seemed surprised and was glad to hear my voice after such a long time. But why suddenly that late and this very evening? Would not next evening be preferable? I replied it had to be tonight, and that it was very important. I promised to explain everything later when we were alone. I knew he would agree.

My mother seemed delighted to see him when he arrived at the door twenty minutes later. Once in the street, I explained that we would not spend the evening together, since I had to attend an important meeting right away. My date with him had been a ruse to get away from home, and I hoped he did not mind doing this for me.

His emotions were written on his face in sequence: astonishment, vexation, and finally dejection. He wanted to know if I had a rival. I swore the meeting had nothing to do with romance and was purely business. I promised to make it up by going out with him the next day, if that was all right with him. I said that unfortunately I was not free to tell him any more.

He seemed relieved and promised to keep our secret, but he also begged me to be careful, whatever I was doing. He must have guessed that I was involved in some plot or other. We kissed and said good night. I felt closer to him than I had at any time in the past.

I arrived at the Café Sainte-Croix in good time and found Jean installed in front of his beer. I sat down next to him and ordered a café-filtre. Stahler and the two other officers were sharing a bottle of wine at their table and were apparently having a good time. I whispered to Jean, "He sure has moved up; he always drank beer before, but now he drinks wine." Jean said softly, "The next move is up to you. You will have to approach him somehow."

I sipped my coffee in silence. I could imagine only one way to attract his attention. I left Jean, walked to Hugo's table, and greeted him like a long-lost friend.

He looked pleasantly surprised to see me, addressed me as his "kleine Hella", and introduced me to his buddies. I was invited to join them and offered a drink. Then, a little more thoughtfully, Hugo asked me if I came often to that café. I said this was my first time and that I was with a friend who was sitting a few tables away.

He glanced over at Jean and asked several questions. I lightly answered that Jean was Belgian, well-to-do, but could speak no German. I made it plain that I was dating him solely for his money. Smiling at this, Hugo insisted that I call him over to our table, adding with a wink, "As long as he doesn't understand German, he won't know what we are talking about, nicht?" I summoned Jean, who cheerfully joined us and went through the round of introductions.

After some small talk, I resumed my distasteful job of wooing Hugo back. I pretended to have missed him since he had left and to be overjoyed to have found him again, adding that I hoped I would see more of him now. Very soon the conceited rake believed that he had made another conquest. Before I left with Jean, Hugo asked when he could see me again, so we arranged a date for the evening after next, at eight o'clock, at the same café.

Outside, Jean, who actually understood quite a bit of German, congratulated me on my performance. He stressed that the Resistance was eager to catch the right man. He also added that he would be away for a few days; he had to be at Namur, at his maquis headquarters. If I had any urgent message for him, I was to phone Franz at his place, as he would be there in the evenings.

Two days later, I arrived at the Café Sainte-Croix at about quarter past eight. Hugo looked worried when I first saw him, but he relaxed as soon as he saw me: "I was afraid you might have changed your mind."

We bantered and joked together and had a few drinks; Hugo ordered supper. I waited for a propitious moment as we sipped freshened drinks, then casually asked him if he found his present work more interesting than his earlier work at Cartography. He said yes, much more interesting, but he was not allowed to talk about it. Then, winking at me as if I were an accomplice, he whispered, half joking, "A secret, y'know."

I pretended to be thrilled and exclaimed brightly, "Oh! You're a *spy,* then? How exciting!" He could not resist a few further remarks, and said no, not a spy, more valuable work than that. Like picking up enemy spies. I sidetracked the conversation at that point, as I did not want to seem too inquisitive. I wondered if I should arrange another date. I said wistfully that it was time for me to leave, but perhaps I could see him again the following evening?

There was regret in his voice when he answered that that was impossible. He had to work. I tried to look disappointed and told him with a pout that I had heard that line before. "You must have a date with another girl. Why else would anyone work at night anyway?"

I must have touched a sensitive spot for he denied the accusation vehemently. Indeed, he was so concerned about clearing himself that he actually blurted out that his job required him to work at night because that was the best time in which to catch enemy agents.

Counter-intelligence officer Hugo Stahler must have been unusually good at his job to have earned London's individual attention. Yet the very fact of his early detection by British Intelligence could be taken as evidence that he was not as smart as he might have been. Obviously I found him dull, vain, tactless, and easy to manipulate. Obviously he considered me just another German girl good only for bedding, to whom he could casually brag of his other exploits.

I gradually elicited some valuable details of what he intended to do the next evening. Put together, the information amounted to a substantial tip. Hugo was to lead a raid on one of the cheap café-hotels along the chaussée de Wavre, where four suspected British women agents were hiding. I pretended to be only vaguely interested and so did not feel able to ask for the hotel's exact location. I hoped that the information I had was enough to act on immediately.

It was late when I glanced at my watch and suggested to Hugo that I phone my parents for permission to stay out later. He readily agreed. At the phone at the far end of the café, I called Jean's number. Franz answered. I told him in very few words about the four girls. Franz wanted to know their names, the number of the street, and more, before launching into what he called a wild-goose chase. I told him curtly not to be so picky and to meet me at the corner of chaussée d'Ixelles and chaussée de Wavre within half an hour, in Jean's truck. He grunted assent, and I hung up. Then I phoned my mother to tell her I was with a group of friends and would be back late, and not to worry. I didn't give her a chance to ask any questions.

When I returned to the table, I told Hugo that my parents were adamant that I return home at once. I tried to look as disappointed as he did. I promised to see him two days later and left, blowing him a kiss full of promise.

I arrived at the rendezvous early to find Franz already there, and the truck parked on a side street. With the scant information we had, he was sceptical of our chances of success. Franz had good reason to be sceptical: the chaussée de Wavre is quite a long road that leads to the town of Wavre some twenty-five kilometres away. We decided that Hugo's hint had indicated the more populated stretch of the road, nearer to the heart of the city. We could do no more than canvass that short section, as that alone would take several hours.

In those days Brussels boasted more cafés per square mile than any other city I know. The word "café" embraces a variety of establishments: the estaminet, a cross between the English pub and the French bistro; the open-air café-terrasse, French-style; the more elaborate tavern and bar; and the café-hotel, which serves drinks downstairs and rents rooms upstairs to transients and one-night lovers. We sought the latter kind of café, pretending to be lovers wanting a room for the night. There were innumerable cafés along the chaussée, but café-hotels were scarcer and spaced well apart. We had been walking in and out of places for well over an hour before we found a likely hiding-place.

The hotel was just another seedy-looking tavern, and once more we went inside to ask for a room. The owner, a short, fat fellow, shook his head. All rooms taken, he said. Then, eyeing us more closely, he mentioned as an afterthought that there was a small room at the end of the upstairs hall that was vacant. He said it was not in very good shape, but if we needed it for only a couple of hours, "it won't make much difference, will it?" He winked broadly at Franz, who quickly accepted and paid for the room. As we climbed the stairs, he whispered to me, "I have a hunch this is it."

The room was actually not much bigger than a large closet, furnished with just a bed and a night table, and very little space in which to move. We agreed that I would remain inside with the door left slightly ajar, while Franz checked the other six rooms we had counted along the corridor. He began to knock systematically on each door, starting with Number 1. Not surprisingly, every time he interrupted the overnight clients in their various activities, he had to endure an avalanche of gross insults, curses, and even threats. He took it all smoothly.

At room Number 5, the room almost directly across from ours, a girl answered the door. She certainly did not look as if she were having an affair, which was immediately suspicious. Franz cast a quick glance inside and glimpsed more girls.

From where I was standing, I too could see them and hear every word they said. Franz said that he had an urgent message for all of them. The girl answered with a slight English accent that she did not expect any messages.

"You are English, aren't you?" asked Franz.

"No," she replied, "I am Belgian. You must have the wrong person." She was about to slam the door in his face but he put his foot in the door.

"Wait! It is a matter of life and death for you and your friends! I came here especially to warn you. The Gestapo knows where you are hiding and may be here to arrest you any moment."

At this point I emerged from our room. I suggested that she let us in rather than continue the discussion in the hall. After consulting her companions, she allowed us to enter the room. Undoubtedly these were the agents, for there were four of them, they all looked and acted English, and every one of them spoke with a tell-tale accent. Yet they persisted in denying their identities, obviously fearing a trap.

When I pointed out to one of them that her accent would give her away, she claimed to be Flemish. I involuntarily laughed. A Flemish accent is itself quite distinctive; and there was no mistaking hers. I said to her, "My poor dear, you wouldn't stand a chance. You can be open with us. We are on your side and are only trying to save your lives." I don't know what sort of an assignment they had been sent on, but they would not have had a chance of surviving their mission with so little training. After a full ten minutes more, they had absorbed the information and decided to accept our advice. We instructed them to gather their few belongings and leave the hotel without drawing attention to themselves, one or two at a time. They had apparently paid a full month's rent in advance—another mistake—so they were free to leave any time as far as the landlord was concerned. We asked them to wait twenty minutes more, then meet us at the next street corner, where we would pick them up and drive them to the Red Cross.

The rescue was a success. Three days later, they were taken from the Red Cross to a Resistance hide-out deep in the Ardennes forest. From there they were to be re-routed to Normandy and eventually returned to England. As far as I know, all went well and they returned safely to their homeland, although I never saw any of them again. I was pleased to have helped save the four girls, but they were not, in my opinion, the stuff of which spies are made.

I still had to cover my tracks with Hugo. Two evenings later when I entered the café, he was scowling. I had hardly sat down before he demanded whether I had mentioned the English girls to anyone. I feigned bewilderment. "What English girls?" He reminded me of the intended raid on the chaussée de Wavre. I pretended to have completely forgotten about it, and asked if anything had happened. Yes, he said, something had happened all right. The four had already escaped before the Gestapo arrived; someone must have tipped them off.

He looked utterly despondent and repeated, "All this work for nothing!" I sympathized and tried to cheer him up. I ordered another drink, and drank to his future successes, but he still looked worried. I turned the conversation, chattering soothingly about nothing but slipping in flattering compliments, acting as if catching spies was simply not in my line of interest. Inevitably Hugo asked me to come to his room with him.

I looked contrite. "Sorry, but not tonight. It would be impossible. I am not well." He sulked and complained that I did this to him every time, making excuses. He wanted to know why.

"You forget, my dear Hugo, that I am a woman. Surely you must know there are times when women are not well. You know what I mean?"

He did. We continued talking and drinking until about ten-thirty. To put him off, I suggested we meet again the following Friday night. It was then that he confided to me that he was being transferred to Normandy before that Friday. Vastly relieved, I said simply that we would surely find some opportunity of meeting again. He suggested leaving a note for me with the café-owner when he was next in Brussels. I agreed, and stoically braced myself when he insisted on kissing me on the lips. I saw it as really a small price to pay for having saved four people from the clutches of the Gestapo.

I never heard from Hugo Stahler after that. I have no doubt that the Resistance took care of him, as intended; but no one ever told me and I never asked. Luck had been on my side again.

6

New Identities

By the autumn of 1941, the greater part of Europe had been under Nazi occupation for eighteen months, and our hopes of liberation by the Allies were dimming with each passing month. When the Germans had invaded Russia in June of 1941, my father and other armchair strategists had exulted and predicted that Germany would soon be faced with a war on two fronts. If Napoleon had been unable to conquer Russia, they reasoned, neither would Hitler succeed. Meanwhile we heard the dismal news of further Nazi victories and advances into Russia day after day. My father and others gradually lost their optimism.

It was in that autumn that Franz and Jean revealed a double surprise to me. They summoned me one evening to an urgent meeting where Jean solemnly announced that I was to undergo small-arms training at last. The training ground was located in the depths of the forêt de Soignes, a chain of dense woods extending for several miles outside Brussels. My lessons would be scheduled for after midnight.

I welcomed the prospect of some action. My exhilaration from helping to rescue the four British agents several weeks earlier was all but extinguished, and my daily routine at home remained uninspiring. Earlier that year, Lily and Sol had finally married and moved into a nearby apartment. By that time, too, business in my father's shop had slowed to the point that I was required only occasionally to check some merchandise, tidy the store, or run an odd errand. I also helped Mother with her cooking and the other household chores.

In these difficult times I knew that my parents would have appreciated some extra income; but finding a job was not only unlikely, but very risky for me, with an identity card marked "ALIEN" and an obviously Jewish name. Although I did not "look Jewish", my mother nonetheless worried that I might be arrested in the street, especially at night. This was one reason my parents did not like me to go out alone in the evenings. I could certainly not be out for a whole night without an acceptable explanation.

I definitely could not tell my parents the truth. The knowledge alone would have placed them in jeopardy. "Only those who can keep their mouths shut stand a chance of surviving," Jean had once told me. "In this game careless talkers do not last long. They end up in the enemy's torture chambers, against the wall, or in a concentration camp." I was duly impressed, but being by nature talkative, I found this secrecy very hard to bear. In retrospect I appreciate that my success in concealing my role in the underground owed a considerable amount to the fact that I knew of many boys and girls, some of them much younger than me, who worked for the Resistance and lived under the same difficult conditions.

I asked Jean if he could suggest an excuse as he knew the problem I faced. His answer was typical: "Necessity is the mother of invention, so use your imagination. But remember, your first training session is scheduled for next Saturday night, and I'll be waiting for you at 2030 hours at the corner of rue Vilain XIV and rue de la Vallée."

After racking my brains that evening, I came up with a fairly plausible story for my family, but I needed a friend's complicity. The girl I chose was a tall, willowy brunette, who had been one of my staunchest supporters in school fights in earlier years. Yvonne lived in our neighbourhood with her widowed mother and I saw her quite often. I arranged with her that I would tell my parents I was staying the night at her place. She readily acquiesced to the conspiracy, in the belief—which I encouraged for simplicity's sake—that I planned to spend the night with Albert. She had always known me as a flirt and showed no surprise. We agreed that if Mother phoned, I would be fast asleep. Thanks to this subterfuge, I was able to keep my appointment.

As I have mentioned, Jean owned a printery and was himself a master printer. He did a certain amount of work for the German authorities, which gave him a good cover and enabled him to keep his truck with the necessary permit. This was an important privilege during the war years since any vehicle could be requisitioned by the occupying forces unless protected by special permit. When I arrived, the truck had been loaded with printing material and machinery to disguise the purpose of our trip.

We left for the forest at dusk. Apart from a few late cyclists here and there and the odd vehicle on the road, the streets were almost deserted. We exchanged a few words but rode for the most part in silence. The night had closed in by the time we reached our destination. Only when we had entered the forest did Jean tell me about my new identity papers.

"They are what we call 'fake authentic'," he said. "You will be assuming the identity of a German woman about your age, who lives in England. She was born in Stuttgart. Both her parents were killed in a car accident. She was disgusted with the Hitler regime, and so left Germany in 1937. She went to England as a student, stayed on, and married an Englishman. At the outbreak of the war she volunteered her services for the Allied cause. Her name—and now yours—is Olga Richter.

"Your cover story, which you will have to know inside out, says among other things that you spent some years with an aunt—now dead—in Belgium, where you learned to speak French."

While I could speak German fluently without a trace of accent, the description made me uneasy. I had never learned to write German properly, and I felt this might give me away. Jean did not seem overly concerned, saying simply that there were many missions that would require only spoken German. "You must keep in mind," he added, "that this document is not for everyday use, only for specific jobs."

"Do you have any such jobs for me right now?"

"Actually we don't. We have decided that you should stay put for the time being, so as to dispel any doubts on the part of your parents. Just relax. Spend some more time with your fiancé and cultivate your friends. You never know when you might need them. When we're ready, either Franz or I will let you know."

We drove on over quiet dirt roads and through the dark tunnel of overhanging trees. Eventually we turned sharply to the left and onto a narrow track, where we bumped along the rest of the way at a snail's pace. Finally we reached a clearing, where we stopped.

It was pitch dark and the mild weather, the peaceful quiet, and the refreshing scents of earth and leafy vegetation soothed my nerves. Jean lit a hurricane lamp that shed an eerie pool of light around us, after

making sure we were absolutely alone. We began to unload the printing gear, gradually clearing the floor of the truck to expose a cleverly
concealed double bottom. Jean removed several boards and piece by
piece pulled out a collection of light firearms. He checked that none
of them was loaded and then began my lessons.

I spent several hours learning to fire a rifle, to handle a revolver and
a sub-machine-gun in various situations, and to load and unload each
piece. I found the large, heavy rifle awkward to hold, but I picked up
the knack of using the service revolver and the Sten gun quite readily.
With both weapons I felt safe and prepared. Jean also showed me how
to throw a hand-grenade and, finally, how to lay dynamite charges for
blowing up a stretch of road or track.

By the first light of dawn my initial training was over and the truck
reloaded. I cannot remember now whether Jean had brought any
sandwiches or beverage, but I remember that I was not hungry or
thirsty—just excited by the experience. With our gear loaded we
waited for broad daylight, when we could merge unobtrusively into
the morning traffic. Jean had given me the documents that established
my new identity. The identity card with my photograph on it looked
perfectly genuine. He also informed me that within the next few days
I would receive further instruction in target practice, with live ammunition, at La Hulpe, a village located some fifteen kilometres south of
the capital. A good friend of his owned large tracts of land there and,
as the hunting season was still open, gunshots in the early morning
would not attract much attention.

In the following week I went through the final course and passed
all tests to my instructor's satisfaction. In lieu of a diploma, he presented me with a loaded hand-gun and a brief address: "You are now
a member of the underground. You will naturally take your orders
from Franz, who is himself answerable directly to London, but you
will both work in close collaboration with the Resistance through me.
And from now on, you will be known by the name of Olga. Forget
Hélène. As for the pistol, do not hesitate to use it if your life is in
danger." I hardly needed to be told.

Over the months the Nazis intensified their harassment of the Jewish
population of Belgium. All Jews were now required by edict to wear a
Star of David at all times. The edict described in minute detail that
the star was to be made of yellow cloth, of a particular size, and
securely sewn, not pinned, to the individual's outer clothes directly
over the heart. I chose to ignore the decree and never once wore that

badge. Despite the traditional significance of the Star of David, the symbol in the eyes of the enemy had become an ignominious stamp. The Nazis intended to brand us like cattle so we could easily be picked up and led to the slaughterhouse. But I was unable to persuade my parents, my sister, or many of my friends to resist as well.

A very large proportion of the Jews living in Belgium at that time were immigrants from eastern Europe who had come to settle there between the two world wars. Unlike American governments, European governments are chary of bestowing their nationality on foreigners, even after many years, sometimes a lifetime, of residence in their countries, and Belgium is no exception. Then, as now, everyone in Europe had to carry an identity card showing name, photo, date and place of birth, and nationality. Cards issued to aliens by the Belgian authorities were a different colour and bore "ALIEN" stamped in bold letters across them. Consequently, Jews carrying such cards were easily identified during identity checks or Gestapo raids and were the first to be arrested.

In the end my reasoning about the star proved to be right, for soon we began to hear of Gestapo patrols rounding up star-bearing Jews at random in the streets of Brussels, herding them into trucks and sending them to Malines (present-day Mechelen), a town some twenty-five kilometres north of the capital. There the Jews were interned in the Caserne Dossin, a military barracks, later to be compressed into cattle trains and transported to various concentration camps.

On learning that even Jews of Belgian nationality were being arrested and incarcerated in Malines, Queen Elizabeth of Belgium, the queen mother, protested to the German high command and was assured that none of her subjects would be mistreated. Soon, however, the Gestapo raids on Jews, whether Belgian or not, dramatically increased. A small detachment of Gestapo satraps in covered trucks would suddenly appear and cordon off a street in the Jewish quarters, then move methodically from house to house, room to room, ordering everyone, men, women, and children, out into the street. Victims were generally not given enough time to gather any belongings or to get fully dressed before being pushed roughly into the waiting trucks. For many of these innocent people the journey ended in the horrors of the concentration camps and the gas chambers.

On the morning that we left the forêt de Soignes just before six, Jean and I happened to witness such a raid from a distance. Portable barriers had been erected at each end of a street block. Between those points there were only three trucks, and six soldiers, two per truck, who rounded up some fifty or sixty adults and some children. I was astounded at the docility of the crowd, given the difference in numbers. The Jews must have known what to expect, but I did not see a single gesture of rebellion or resistance. I was ashamed of such apathy.

Jean must have sensed my emotions for he drove on without a word. We both knew, through the underground network, that many Jews had been approached by members of the Resistance and invited to join them in the maquis. They were offered arms and ammunition, and even bottles of sulphuric acid with which to defend themselves. All but a handful had declined the offer, on what grounds I still cannot imagine. They may have been the victims of religious fanaticism, paralyzing fear, or sheer cowardice.

As part of their ghastly obsession with the "Jewish problem", the Nazis indulged in other tricks, such as sending out summonses to Jewish homes or to people with Jewish-sounding names. The recipients were ordered to report to the Caserne Dossin at Malines within forty-eight hours. Those who refused to obey found themselves caught in a desperate game of hide-and-seek. Some changed their identity with the connivance of friendly officials, and others found refuge with Gentile friends or in other hiding-places that, though safe, were by no means foolproof. Of course the Germans had decreed that anyone harbouring Jews without reporting them immediately to the authorities was also liable to imprisonment or deportation.

Some of our friends managed to find shelter with Gentile families, but as all Jewish bank accounts were frozen by the Nazis, these Jews could only throw themselves on the mercy of their Gentile hosts, hoping to repay their debt after the war. Quite a number of these Gentiles accordingly became paid informers reporting to the Gestapo. I learned the grim details of such vile traffic at first hand. For this service informers collected a paltry forty francs after the arrest of the victim.

My parents and others in the family finally realized the implications of wearing the Star of David, and they gave up wearing it, as did many others. However, our family was well known in the neighbourhood, either personally or through our business, so the danger of our being arrested by the Gestapo nonetheless grew with each passing day.

In an attempt to avoid the inevitable, my father closed the shop, locked up the apartment, and took us all to the country to live on a farm. But after a couple of months, growing restless and knowing that the Gestapo raided villages as well as towns, he decided to take a chance and return to Brussels. Soon after our return, he found a

Gentile partner, a man named Oscar Estournier, a tailor by trade, who moved in with his wife to run the business for half the profits. Estournier had been recommended by his brother, who knew my father well. Estournier accepted the partnership on the condition that he himself be allowed to carry on tailoring at our place.

As the Estourniers had no children, they were content to establish their living quarters downstairs behind the shop, while we remained in the upstairs apartment. My mother, who had a sure instinct for judging people, did not approve of our new partners, for she considered them too greedy. Father only shrugged and claimed he had no alternative in such troubled times.

The summer months passed with little news from either Franz or Jean. During that period I saw a lot more of Albert, and we eventually became lovers, although I still could not look upon him as my future husband. I did not feel completely at ease with him, possibly because I knew I did not truly love him. I also balked at the idea of marriage, which I saw as a threat to my cherished freedom. The fact that Albert had a steady job as a furrier and would have been a good provider for a family did not enter into my thinking at that age. My mother, however, felt our marriage would control my unruly nature and protect me automatically, as a Belgian subject by marriage, from Nazi persecution.

I wished I could tell her about my newly bestowed German identity, which protected me more than marriage to Albert ever could. But I held my tongue. As the weeks went by, parental pressure mounted until I felt cornered. I finally agreed to marry Albert, who was certainly willing enough, but I insisted on a "mariage blanc," in case the marriage proved a failure. These marriages were in all respects legal, but the parties agreed that either spouse could ask to dissolve the union at the end of the war if he or she so desired. The necessary document was drawn up by a lawyer and signed by all parties. Many such weddings had recently taken place between Belgian Gentiles and Jews to save the Jewish spouse from threatened deportation. Albert consented to the formality, hoping, as he repeated, that in time I would become a contented and loving wife to him. We rented a furnished room in an adjacent street to serve as our official home. Otherwise everything went on very much as before.

When Franz and Jean heard about the wedding they were furious. They complained that it would drastically restrict my movements and curtail my underground activities. I responded that I had had to do it to pacify my parents, and I assured them that I intended to carry on my underground work just as before.

Barely a week after the wedding, my brand-new husband received a summons to report to the Dossin barracks at Malines. The summons had arrived at his parents' home, so I felt that he would be wise to ignore it since he did not officially live there any longer. He disagreed with me because, as a Belgian subject, he was sure he would be released in a matter of days, as he said others had been. I knew he would not come back if he reported to Malines, but I could not shake his confidence. His words as he blew me a last kiss were, "We'll have dinner together when I get back." I sincerely hoped he was right.

. One week passed, and there was no news. As there was no way that anyone could communicate with Malines internees, both our families simply had to wait. It was not until three weeks later that a Gentile acquaintance brought me a postcard from Albert, addressed to him but written to me. It had apparently been thrown from the transport train as it passed through the countryside and some charitable soul had picked it up and mailed it. It said, "Dear Hélène, I should have listened to you. Hope to see you again soon."

His abrupt disappearance affected me deeply, more than I would have thought possible. Feelings and memories of him in the past months washed over me in my emptiness. My hatred for the invaders strengthened my resolve to do everything I could, by fair means or foul, to help in their annihilation.

Soon after Albert's arrest I found that my new status as the wife of a Belgian made no difference to the Nazis, to whom I was the same Jewish alien I had been before my marriage. For everyday use, for obtaining ration cards, a job, or new lodgings, I desperately needed a safe identity as a Belgian Gentile. After long and frustrating attempts to get one, I was introduced by my brother-in-law to someone who knew a patriotic clerk at city hall willing to issue a "fake authentic" card to me. To do this, he needed a bona fide card from another woman and a photo of me. So I had to find a woman willing to lend me her own card.

I could not use Yvonne's card because we lived too near each another. After some thought I remembered Andrée Fiévez, an old friend from pre-war days, who lived near Genval, just outside Brussels. We had been very close as young girls but I had lost contact with her when she had married several years before.

She was delighted to hear from me and invited me to have coffee at her home. I found her alone with her little girl, who was three years old at the time. She told me that her husband was a prisoner of war in Germany, and we chatted for a while about our happy schooldays of so long ago. Over second cups of coffee I haltingly explained that I needed a document that would disguise both my name and my background, and she immediately offered me her identity card, assuring me that she could easily get a replacement. Her gesture touched me deeply; overcome with tears and gratitude, I embraced her.

My new card in the name of Andrée Fiévez bore my actual birthdate, December 24, 1920, and stated that my birthplace was Ostend. With my two new identities as Olga Richter and Andrée Fiévez, I finally felt secure and free to move around. I waited a long time for a signal from either Franz or Jean. Finally, early in the autumn of 1942, I heard from Franz. At last he had a mission for me.

7

Into the
Wolf's Lair

As usual I met Franz at Jean's apartment. He told me that he had developed a plan to infiltrate the Gestapo headquarters on avenue Louise and that he would need my help. The latter part of his remark alarmed and then puzzled me. Although the Gestapo building was practically around the corner from my home, I had always been careful to avoid it as much as possible. When I said so, Franz smoothly continued to outline his scheme.

"The head of the Gestapo and his assistant have their morning break every day around ten o'clock at the Café Louise, porte Louise. They usually have breakfast or a snack there, and my informant confirms that they always sit in the same corner, near the window.

"Your role will be to patronize the same café, where you will have your coffee and rolls every morning around a quarter to ten. You are to sit at a table as near those officers as possible so they can see you easily. With your looks and charm it shouldn't take too long before you attract their interest. It may take a week or two, maybe three, before you manage to start a conversation with them. When you do, you will introduce yourself as Olga Richter. At the first convenient opportunity, you will mention your fiancé, Franz Boehler—me—a sergeant who works at the Todt and is not very happy there. You'll mention my knowledge of languages, which should interest them further, especially as I know they do not speak French themselves. After that we'll play it by ear."

I thought the idea of acting as such a pawn was preposterous. But Franz was a patient man and a good schemer. He reminded me of my hatred of the Boches and my desire to defeat them. And he stressed that if he could gain entry to the Gestapo, he would be of the greatest possible help to London, and to both Jews and Gentiles. I was the only person he knew who might be capable of getting him in. This was his last chance before London either recalled him or sent him to join the maquis.

Before he had finished speaking, I realized that he had obtained my German papers with just that mission in mind. He said the idea of providing me with a German identity was part of a plan he had conceived with the approval of the Resistance to enable me to contact members of vital German units, such as the Gestapo. I would have to overcome my natural repugnance to Gestapo personnel as I had my aversion to Hugo Stahler. After lengthy arguments, I consented to help.

Franz met me at ten-thirty the next morning outside the Café Louise. From the street he indicated the two men seated near the window and in a low voice briefed me on them. The taller of the two was dark-haired and wore glasses and looked about forty. This was Mueller, the chief of the Brussels Gestapo. The other was his assistant, Schwenke, a much younger man, blond, and somewhat shorter than his superior. Now that I could recognize them both, I was ready to embark on "Operation Attraction".

When I entered the Café Louise the next morning, my quarries were already settled in their accustomed corner, having breakfast. I had dressed carefully in my pearl grey tailor-made suit and a white silk blouse with lace frills at the neck and cuffs, my only pair of silk stockings—a present from Mother—and high-heeled shoes. I had decided not to wear a hat. I casually sat down at a nearby table facing them and summoned the waiter for coffee and rolls. While I strained to hear their conversation, I spread out my newspaper and pretended to read it. Now and again I raised my head to look towards the door as if expecting someone, but actually scrutinizing the two Nazis intently. Not until I had finished my rolls and was sipping the dregs of my coffee did Mueller and Schwenke begin to discuss me.

I overheard the younger of the two men say: "That young woman over there seems to be all by herself. And quite a looker too." I did not catch the older man's words, but again the younger one said, looking straight at me this time: "What a pretty sight! I wonder if she is waiting for someone."

This startled me but I smiled in their direction and tried to convey by my smile that I understood what they had been saying. Schwenke must have realized I understood them, for he looked very surprised.

"Well, I'll be damned!" he exclaimed. I was seized with sudden panic as I saw him deliberately rise and walk towards my table. What if he arrested me? Maybe this was the end.

"Excuse me, Fräulein, but I am under the impression that you understand German."

Much relieved by the question, I replied with what I fancied was a touch of Teutonic arrogance, "Natürlich, ich bin doch Deutsche" (Naturally, I am German of course). With a frank air of disappointment I added that I had been expecting a friend, but he had not come.

"In that case may I invite you to our table, Fräulein?"

I pretended to be much honoured, and accepted with a smile, but my heart was in my mouth. Things were moving much faster than I had anticipated, too fast, and I did not feel ready for the test. Mueller turned to me, his face radiating false bonhomie, as Schwenke helped seat me at their table: "A pretty girl like you should not be sitting by herself, all alone."

I laughed heartily, as if much impressed by his awkward gallantry. I knew from experience that my laughter appealed to men, and indeed, it seemed to please the two Gestapo chiefs, for they settled down to a very amiable chat with me. They introduced themselves, and I gave my name as Olga Richter, recently arrived from Stuttgart. They offered me a cup of coffee. Answering a question from Mueller, I told them that I had come to Brussels to join my fiancé, who had just been posted to the Todt.

Schwenke, his eyes all over me, asked, "How come you have not joined the forces, like the other girls your age?"

I pouted, and replied that I didn't think I would be very successful in the army, under other women. "I don't get on well with women," I said. "Even as a little girl I preferred playing with boys, and fought with the girls. But I got on fine with the men." At that they laughed loudly.

"Then what do you do for a living?" Mueller pursued.

"Oh, I am looking for a job at the moment. You know, I can speak and write French fluently. Before the war I spent some years here, living with an aunt of mine. My fiancé knows French thoroughly, too, as well as several other languages. I always tell him his talents are wasted at the Todt, repairing bridges and things. It is a pity, because he could be of so much more service to the Vaterland."

They had both been listening attentively. Mueller spoke first: "Tell your friend to come and see me. Our section pays well, and there are all sorts of privileges. If he speaks French, I think his place could be with us." He extracted a paper from his wallet and asked me for Franz's full name. When he had written it down, he signed the paper and handed it to me, saying, "This is his pass. Without it he will not be allowed in. My office is on the eighth floor. Tell him to come to see me as soon as he can. If we find him suitable, we will obtain his transfer."

Schwenke, still mentally stripping me, spoke again. "I think your friend is very lucky to have such a good looker all to himself." I acknowledged the lewd compliment with a smile.

Mueller glanced at his watch and jumped up. "Mein Gott! We are late! I have an important meeting; we must be off! Fräulein Olga, it was a pleasure meeting you. I hope we shall see you again soon." They saluted and were gone.

Simultaneously exhilarated and weak in the knees, I could hardly wait to break the news to Franz. I phoned the barracks and left a coded message that I urgently wished to see him that same evening at Jean's place.

When I called at the apartment later, Franz was there, looking thoughtful. Impatient to see his reaction, I produced the paper from my purse and handed it to him, saying simply, "Mission accomplished." He gaped at the pass, turned it over several times, and looked at me, much bewildered, asking how the devil I had obtained it. Even after I had recounted the scene in detail, he shook his head muttering, "I cannot believe it! This is simply incredible!" At last he remembered to congratulate me and promised to let me know how he fared with Mueller. Then we rehearsed the fine points of our cover stories regarding our alleged relationship.

I saw him again a week later. He had been interviewed, examined, found suitable, and accepted as a Gestapo officer. So far, so good. I wished him luck in his new undercover position.

In the meantime I was still living at home. We pooled our rations, as did most families, and with a few extra items from the black market, we managed to get by. However, Father's income from the business was gradually shrinking, and the Estourniers were now running the store themselves. Officially they were now considered the owners of the business, since Jewish ownership was no longer recognized by the Nazis, and the Estourniers let us know that they did not want any extra help. Father had in effect become a silent partner of his own business.

Desperate to help support myself, I had been job-hunting without success. As I possessed no special skills, my prospects were naturally limited. Those firms most willing to hire unskilled help were those working for the Germans, and I flatly refused to seek employment with them. In fact the Nazis often raided the factories for both male and female workers to be shipped to Germany as forced labour. So I could not apply there.

In October I was finally hired by the Salvation Army, of all places, as an assistant in the maternity ward, which was really a home for unwed mothers and delinquent girls. The pay was poor, but the noon-day meals, which were the main daily repast in Belgium, were included. I felt the job would help my parents' finances slightly and perhaps provide me with a hide-out in an emergency. And I liked handling babies.

I was hired on a Monday and instructed to report for work the following Wednesday. That Monday night, I met Franz again at his urgent request. He wanted to tell me that he had been assigned an office all to himself at Gestapo headquarters and had been put in charge of espionage and arrests. He looked pensive for a moment, or pretended to, and then suddenly announced that he wanted me to be his secretary there.

The ensuing meeting was a stormy one. I told him that I had no intention of giving up my much-needed new job at the Salvation Army before I had even started it. Franz's offer seemed wild and unnecessarily risky for both of us, besides being wholly impractical. And while I spoke proper German, I certainly could not write it, which hardly made me Gestapo secretarial material. I had already done my part in making it possible for him to infiltrate the Gestapo, and that was as much as I would do.

He begged me to allow him to explain how important my help would be. Written German, he said, would not be required, as I would be working exclusively for him. Since he would be checking the lists of all those to be arrested for interrogation, deportation, or execution, our working together as a team could save many lives. Alone he would be severely handicapped. As usual he played on my emotions, and I had to agree finally that the job was a vital one. But for my parents' sake I refused to give up my new Salvation Army job. Eventually we reached a compromise. On my two half-days off from the

Salvation Army every week, I would report for duty at his Gestapo office. He did not offer me any pay, and I did not ask for any.

The following day was Tuesday, and I found myself free to do as I pleased. The morning air was crisp, and the warming sun promised perfect autumn weather, so I decided to take a long walk along avenue Louise all the way to the bois de la Cambre. In those days the avenue was bordered by tall chestnut trees, with a broad footpath down the middle for "le footing". I had walked only a short distance along the path, enjoying the leafy trees and cool sunlight, when a car pulled over to the curb beside me. I glanced in the window and recognized with a sudden shock a Gestapo uniform inside. It was Mueller. I saw myself being arrested. My blood froze.

He greeted me cordially, all smiles. "Well, well, if it isn't Fräulein Olga herself! And how are you, on this fine morning?"

I answered very well, thank you, and managed to smile amiably in return. Thus encouraged, he continued: "I thought you would come and visit me. A pretty girl must not hide!"

I mumbled some excuse and, regaining some poise, asked, "By the way, how is my fiancé making out?"

As if he had forgotten all about Franz, he said, "Oh! Your fiancé! That's right. Yes, he is doing very well. Charming fellow. Very zealous. Never late." As an afterthought, he added, "But why not come with me? We'll give him a surprise, nicht?"

I decided it would not be wise to refuse. He invited me to sit beside him in the car. I climbed in but felt acutely uncomfortable, fearful that someone would recognize me, riding cheek by jowl with a Gestapo officer, although our trip was short. In those days of restricted transportation for civilians, all cars were conspicuous, especially the luxurious Gestapo staff cars.

I cannot describe the fear I felt as I stepped inside the dreaded Gestapo building that morning. Not until that moment had I really appreciated my position, a Belgian Jewish girl in the role of a German Fräulein, flanked by Obersturmbannführer Mueller, colonel in charge of the Brussels Gestapo, walking quietly past guard after guard through the long hallways and greeted by the rapid fire of "Heil Hitler" salutes and clicking heels.

Centuries later, or so those five minutes seemed, when we reached Franz's office on the eighth floor, I felt a little calmer. Mueller opened the door and shouted to an astonished Franz, with exaggerated geniality, "Look who is here to see you! None other than your own little Freundin; she was pining for you, you lucky fellow!" When my colleague did not display any immediate enthusiasm, he went on, "But if you do not want her, just let me know. I am always ready to enjoy a masterpiece!"

Franz did not look at all amused. "But, Herr Oberst, I really don't have time for her now. I hardly have time to eat, I am so flooded with work. Olga dear, please go away. I will see you tonight."

Much amused, Mueller turned to me, still playing the jovial host. "Come along with me, my dear. I'll show you my office. We can sit and have a quiet chat together. I am not in the mood for work just now anyway."

He grandly ushered me into his own office—which he shared with the absent Hauptsturmführer Schwenke—several doors away from Franz's. After waving me to a chair, he produced a bottle of liqueur and two glasses. Pouring, he said, "Let us drink first to the Führer, and to victory!" In the time I took to finish my first glass, he must have gulped at least five. I noticed his glistening eyes with growing alarm and tried to look at my ease. Mueller looked me over longingly and asked abruptly, "What would you say if I asked you to be my secretary? After all, girls nowadays are busy at some job or other— army, office, factory, or whatever." When I remained silent, desperately trying to think of a convincing excuse, he said, "You know, I find it strange that you do not work for the Vaterland. I think your friend spoils you and wants you all to himself."

I found my excuse while he was talking. "I am truly sorry, Herr Mueller, but I am not able to accept your generous offer. You see, the truth is that I have a heart condition, and my doctor forbids me to work too hard. I cannot be employed in a job that would involve me too emotionally. So I cannot hold a steady job." I paused, pretending to think. "But I'll tell you what I am willing to do, if you agree. I could work a few hours a week helping Leutnant Boehler with his office work. I wouldn't want any salary. After all, since he keeps me, it's only fair that I should help him, if only part-time."

Mueller nodded approvingly at this offer. Then he immediately summoned Franz, and repeated it to him. Franz naturally agreed this was a great idea and promised that he would be ready for me to start within the next few days. Fortunately Mueller did not hear my sigh of relief.

And so, with Franz I had penetrated the Gestapo, as an unpaid part-time assistant to "Leutnant" Franz Boehler, Gestapo officer in charge of espionage and arrests, himself a British agent. Henceforth I would have to live with the ever-present fear of being found out and subjected to the frightful tortures and death reserved for secret agents caught by the Gestapo. But another frightful ordeal, quite different from the one I imagined, was soon to make a very terrible change in my life.

8

Inside
the Gestapo

I enjoyed my work at the maternity ward of the Salvation Army. Mme Van Keppel, my boss, officially known as Major Van Keppel, had taken a liking to me, and allowed me to take two half-days off a week. She believed I was working part-time at a store to bolster my meagre earnings, when I was actually spending those afternoons working in Franz's Gestapo office. In his new capacity, Franz was entitled to an apartment and a car of his own. I paid my first visit to his lodgings soon after he was installed, not so much out of curiosity as to discuss in detail the implications of his new position and mine. I was eager, I told him, to become actively involved in various operations to save people from the Gestapo, although the details of how I would help carry out such an aim were very vague in my mind.

Franz's new job was to consider stacks of briefs on individuals who were about to be arrested, or had already been, mostly for political reasons. Some of these were well-known members of the Resistance who faced torture and the firing squad if captured. Saving those not yet arrested would logically be our first priority. Once they had been warned and hidden if possible, the Resistance would try to help them escape to England by one of several routes.

The thought of my parents' precarious safety was foremost in my mind, and when escape routes were mentioned, I could not resist broaching the subject. I hoped to see them escape to Switzerland, as they spoke both French and German, and Franz approved of the idea. He emphasized, however, that I would need their consent. If they refused the offer to escape when I first asked them, they must know nothing more about our network. Despite Franz's warning, I was so excited at the prospect of seeing Mother and Father safe that I could hardly wait to break the good news to them.

Since my father's virtual retirement from his business, my parents felt it necessary to remain in their apartment at all times for fear of being recognized by roving street patrols. When they did occasionally leave home, they were never out for long. My mother had given up all social visits and had curtailed her once daily shopping trips to once a week. Father went out for a few minutes every evening to buy his newspaper and cigarettes at a kiosk two blocks away. With his strong Jewish features, we knew that even these short trips presented risks. Fortunately I was able to leave home in the mornings and return in the evenings, as my Gentile papers and my appearance lent me confidence. But for both my parents, the strain of being confined together week after week, and month after month, was taking its toll. Father had become more irritable and argumentative than ever, and his moods in turn frayed Mother's own shortened temper. They quarrelled increasingly over trivial matters, and the various tensions frustrated me greatly. Despite all the bickering, we cared deeply for one another and I was all the more determined to help them escape.

One evening while Mother was cooking dinner and Father was reading his newspaper in the kitchen, I bluntly asked him whether he would like to leave for Switzerland. With a rather quizzical smile, he asked how I thought this could be done. I said that someone I knew could arrange for him and Mother to be taken there. He immediately wanted to know the man's name and how much money he expected. He was sceptical and sarcastic when I answered that no money would be involved: "For heaven's sake, Father! He works for the Resistance. It would be a favour!"

"And what part would *you* play in all this?" asked my father, still looking very doubtful. I had known the man for years, I said calmly, and could vouch for his reliability.

Mother had been listening quietly from the stove. "I think Hélène's idea is worth considering. As far as I'm concerned, I'd like nothing better than to get away from here and live in a free country."

Father, however, continued to raise objections. How did I know they would not be arrested on the way? "If I stay here," he argued, "we probably have a better chance of not being discovered by the Boches."

"Father, the Gestapo are arresting more and more Jews all the time now. Sooner or later they could come for you, too. Then it would be too late."

"You're overreacting, Hélène. The Boches couldn't possibly search every nook and cranny of the city, and, besides, the war can't last forever. I don't see that it's all that likely they'll come after us here."

Father was as stubborn as a mule. He insisted he would have no guarantee that they would make it safely all the way to the Swiss border, and he simply did not want to take the risk. He shook open his newspaper again decisively, ending the discussion. There was nothing more I could do. Overwrought, I burst into tears while Mother took me in her arms and tried to console me. She knew I had wanted to help.

I realize now how my father must have seen me then, as a little girl who still needed parental guidance and supervision, and not as a young adult whose judgement he could trust. My mother accepted that I could look after myself, and I know she trusted me implicitly. I am sure now that she suspected I was occasionally involved in secret anti-German activities of some kind, but she wisely never asked me any direct questions.

A few weeks after this episode my mother told me that she had given my Salvation Army address to Mlle Baudhuin, our landlady, so that she could contact me in case of any emergency. No one was supposed to know where I worked, but Mlle Baudhuin was a most trustworthy person, and Mother's decision was a sensible one.

As the days passed, my mother grew increasingly apprehensive. Estournier had decided to tailor uniforms for German officers, and the comings and goings of these clients at all hours were most unsettling to my family. For reasons that I have never understood, my father's faith in his partner remained unshakeable, and this eventually led him to make a fatal blunder. One day he disclosed to the tailor that he had hidden our family jewels and money in the coal cellar, where no one but he, he said, would be able to find them. When Mother learned of the indiscretion, she was furious. She considered the Estourniers only too capable of reporting us to the Gestapo for the sake of our hard-earned savings, but Father merely scoffed at what he called her imagination.

I was very worried about my parents, for I had seen long Gestapo lists of Jews recently rounded up. I had also been able to surreptitiously observe some of them being escorted to the basement of the building, where they were usually locked up for a day or two before their transfer to Malines. The Gestapo office girls were forbidden anywhere near the stairs to the cellars beneath. In my case I had to also avoid being noticed by someone who might have recognized me as a Jewish girl named Hélène Moszkiewiez. But the sight of these helpless people, my people, being led away to their doom upset me tremendously. Standing at the elevator, waiting to be taken to the eighth floor, I would inwardly tremble, reminded yet again just how near I stood to the same fate.

Monday, December 7, 1942, is a date that I will never forget, as it was the first day of my most serious troubles. Franz had driven me to his apartment, where I was to pick up an attaché case. Inside were four service revolvers and two boxes of ammunition that had been stolen from the Germans and were now destined for the use of the Resistance. Franz had asked me to store the case and its contents for several days, while he would be out of town. He would retrieve it as soon as he returned. I had suggested instead that I make two trips home in order to carry the revolvers and ammunition separately so that I could leave the bulky case. The only safe place I knew at home was an old-fashioned chest of drawers in my room. The bottom drawer had been assigned to my exclusive use, so that is where I hid the guns, under some lingerie.

Four days later, on Friday, December 11, 1942, the blow fell. At about four in the afternoon, I was busy at the maternity ward when Major Van Keppel called me: "There is a lady asking to see you. She says it is urgent. She seems quite upset."

Mlle Baudhuin had come all the way across town to see me. "Madame Hélène, do not return home." She was crying, and spoke haltingly. "The Gestapo were there this afternoon and took away your poor parents. I think they know there is also a daughter living there, and they will certainly pick you up too."

I broke down and collapsed, sobbing. One is never prepared for the worst, no matter how imminent it has been. Only some minutes later was I able to ask Mlle Baudhuin for more details. In a low voice she confided that she strongly suspected Estournier of having a part in my parents' arrest. When the Gestapo had called, he had been the one to knock on Father's door, shouting, "It's me, Estournier." My parents would naturally never have answered the door unless they recognized the caller's voice. When Father had unsuspectingly opened it, he had found himself facing two Gestapo men. Mother had been out shopping at the time and had unfortunately returned while the Gestapo were still there, ransacking the apartment. She must not have noticed the car ominously parked near the house. By the time she realized her mistake, she had already reached the stairs. She turned to run away, but Estournier was there to bar her escape.

In a loud voice that could be heard by the Nazis upstairs, he said, "I cannot let you go now, Madame Moszkiewiez. If I do, the soldiers will take me as hostage instead."

Mlle Baudhuin had watched from her window as my mother was marched to the car. She said that one of the Boches had shoved Mother and shouted at her to hurry her along, whereupon she had swiftly turned and slapped the bully's face. The brute had been so taken aback by this show of spirit that he had not reacted against her at all. Crying, Mlle Baudhuin said, "Your mother was a courageous woman, Madame Hélène, you can be proud of her."

Major Van Keppel, who by now had heard the news, did not feel that it would be safe for me to remain in her ward any longer, in case the Boches looked for me there. She sent me to the Salvation Army headquarters on rue Haute, where I was given a job and a small bedroom of my own to sleep in until the danger had passed. Mlle Baudhuin saved my life that day, and for that I will always be grateful to her.

When I was settled in at the Salvation Army quarters I suddenly remembered the hand-guns I had hidden at home only a few days earlier, and which Franz had not yet claimed. If the Gestapo found them, my parents would certainly be shot, following torture. I was panic-stricken. I had to contact Franz immediately at any cost.

He was not at home when I banged on his door. In a panic I ran to the Gestapo offices, although the hour was very late. The guard refused to admit me until I gave him Franz's name. He phoned his office, and fortunately Franz was there working overtime. He ordered the guard to let me through.

Looking grim, he agreed we had to act quickly. As our home was so near to Gestapo headquarters, Franz suspected that my parents might have been brought in and confined to the basement below us until the next day.

"Wait for me," he said, "and I'll see if they're there." He was gone for what seemed like hours. When he reappeared, he looked relieved. Through a judas hole in the transit room he had seen them, though they had not noticed him. "If they had been under any particular suspicion whatsoever—or if the guns had been found—they would have been locked up in the other cellar, where they keep political prisoners before interrogation."

This news lifted my spirits greatly, for it gave me hope that I might see my parents when the war was over. As for the guns, there were two possibilities: either the Gestapo had not found them, or, if they had, they had neglected to report the find. Franz agreed that there was no time to waste, and that I should retrieve the four revolvers that evening from my parents' apartment, if they were still there. He would drive me there around midnight as the chances of meeting the Gestapo at that late hour were much reduced. In fact they usually avoided entering premises in the middle of the night.

Just before midnight we arrived at the corner of rue Vilain XIV. The street was deserted. As I stepped out of the car, Franz placed his Luger in my hand. "If Estournier tries anything funny," he said coolly, "or wants to make trouble, shoot him. Don't even hesitate. Now hurry. I'll wait here."

I opened the front door with my spare key as soundlessly as possible, feeling like a thief in my parents' house. I was halfway up the stairs when Estournier, who must have heard me, came out in the hall. He gave a cry of surprise when he saw me and then, recovering, snarled, "What are *you* doing here at this time of night? You are not allowed to enter that apartment. The door's been sealed by the Gestapo. You're lucky to still be at large."

I quickly descended the stairs and whispered to him urgently that I wanted to have a word with him. I pulled out the gun and, keeping it pointed at him, ordered him back into the shop. When I had followed him inside I ripped the telephone cord off the wall with my free hand. Now wide-eyed and pale, Estournier looked terrified.

His wife came out of her bedroom in search of him, saw me with the gun, and began to tremble. Before she could open her mouth, I told her, "If you yell or make the slightest noise, I will kill your husband right here, on the spot. Now," I said, turning to him sharply, "you, espèce de salaud, are going to walk upstairs, in front of me, and open that sealed door with your own hands. Now move, and don't forget your life is now in my hands."

Like most informers, he was a coward, and he meekly obeyed my orders. The place was a sorry mess. Those gangsters had ransacked our apartment very thoroughly and stolen every portable thing of value, including my mother's fur coat, her winter clothing, my new shoes, and a brand-new overcoat I had worn only twice. I went straight to

the chest of drawers. The drawers of the chest gaped wide open, most
of their contents dumped all over the floor. However, my own bottom
drawer was closed. Nothing inside seemed to have been touched; the
revolvers were exactly where I had hidden them, with the ammunition. It seemed like a miracle. I guessed that one of the looters must
have been interrupted before he had had time to open the last drawer.

Estournier had been watching me; when he saw the guns, which I
dropped into the bag I had brought with me for the purpose, his eyes
almost popped out of their sockets. Now subdued and apprehensive,
he spoke in a whisper. "You are playing with fire, you know."

"That's right, you dirty bastard, but this fire is meant for the likes
of you. These guns are going to the Resistance, who will surely take
care of you, if I don't. But I'll settle with you, sooner or later, make no
mistake about that."

He looked petrified at this and did not say another word. I gave
him a final warning: "You stay here until I have gone. Don't move." I
left him standing there, ran downstairs, and, closing the door behind
me, rushed with my loot back to the car where Franz was waiting for
me impatiently.

I returned to the house the following evening, this time accompanied by my sister and her husband, who lived around the corner under
assumed names. We had met earlier in the day and held a family
council during which we had decided to call at the house around half
past nine to dig up Father's cache in the cellar before the Estourniers
had a chance to find it. Both Lily and my brother-in-law knew nothing about my underground activities until a few days before the Liberation, and I did not mention my visit the previous night. At the house
I sent both of them straight to the cellar, telling them I would look
after the Estourniers to keep them out of the way. Lily thought this a
dangerous and nearly impossible task for me alone, but I insisted. She
did not know, of course, that I was carrying a gun. When Estournier
answered my knock, he sprang back in terror at the sight of me, no
doubt certain that I had already come to wreak the vengeance I had
promised him. With my gun pointed at him through my coat pocket,
I stepped into the room and closed the door behind me. I noticed with
relief that the phone had not yet been reconnected.

Very calmly I addressed both of them, so that they could not have
missed the seriousness of my words: "If you value your lives, you will
both stay where you are, and not move a hair, until my brother-in-law
has found the treasure Father buried in the cellar." I maliciously

wanted them to believe that they had missed their chance to seize a sizeable fortune.

Some twenty minutes later, the cache had been found, the box of valuables removed, and in no time we had left the house. My sister kept asking how I had managed to subdue the Estourniers so successfully, and I told her this was not the time for long explanations. The treasure we had recovered consisted of only my mother's rings and about thirty thousand francs in American dollars. It was not much, but we intended to keep it for our parents for their return.

From that day on I was obsessed with the idea of freeing my parents from the Malines detention centre before their certain deportation to a concentration camp, when it would be too late to help them. The wildest schemes ran through my head. The Dossin barracks held hundreds of Jews and were guarded by only a handful of soldiers. A small contingent of determined maquisards, properly armed, could have overcome the guards with little trouble, and freed the hundreds of prisoners. I reasoned that since my principal mission in the underground was to save as many victims as possible from the enemy's grip, I had every right to ask the Resistance for help and support.

When I submitted my rough plan to Jean, he was quick to point out its weaknesses. For one thing, he said, the Resistance had neither enough men nor sufficient equipment and facilities to handle a crowd of some four hundred freed detainees, including older people and young children. And to leave such a helpless crowd to its own devices after freeing them would only invite an immediate massacre by the Nazis. Even if a number of them managed to escape such a fate, their chances of eluding the Gestapo a second time were slim. And to sacrifice so many people for the sake of only one couple, he added, would be unconscionable. He reminded me of my commitment to London and the underground, which required obedience above all else.

Although I had to admit that that particular plan would be unworkable, others kept rushing through my mind. I had to find some way of liberating my parents. When another idea struck me later that day, I worked on it feverishly until late into the night. By the following morning I had perfected it to the point where I was ready to carry it out. I had no intention of allowing anyone to discourage me, so this time I kept my own counsel. The plan was a daring one that could easily have blown up in my face. It would involve Mueller.

Obersturmbannführer Mueller was an unremarkable man of about forty years, of mediocre intelligence, who, had he been a civilian, would have passed completely unnoticed in a crowd. The feature I remember most was his eyes; they were of indeterminate colour, steely, and absolutely unsmiling. Even when he did rarely smile, his eyes remained cold. His manners were typical of the lower-middle-class German Nazi who had risen through Gestapo ranks to a position of power: he was arrogant, harsh, and brutal to the lower ranks, servile to his superiors, and completely dedicated to his job. He was married, had one daughter, and, from what I could gather, seemed to be a good husband and fond father. Above all else, he was entirely devoted to Hitler and hated Jews fanatically. Where Jews were concerned, he was a merciless automaton whose sole aim was to capture as many of them as possible and ship them away for disposal.

He had one weakness that was easily detected: vulnerability to the opposite sex. With German Aryan women, he pretended to be the perfect gentleman, polite, attentive, and warmly protective. He considered the younger ones in particular as objects of desire and enjoyment to be handled with care. He treated me as if I belonged in that category.

After I had successfully parried his first subtle attempts to seduce me, our relationship resolved itself into an amiable one within the context of our relative business positions. For a while this understanding served my purpose well enough. I sensed that he still desired me in an avuncular sort of way, and with a certain amount of respect. Perhaps I reminded him of his own daughter. This last idea finally emboldened me to act as I did.

Early one morning, eight days after my parents' arrest, I was alone in my office, filing away some papers, at a time when I knew Mueller was alone in his. Having made up my mind, I seized a file and walked to the door. There I hesitated, quaking with fear, and had to return to my chair and sit down in a cold sweat. What I intended to do suddenly seemed so far-fetched and unreal that my head was spinning. What if my request were turned down, I asked myself, and I were arrested for further questioning? That would certainly be my end, and probably that of Franz as well. But I could not let my parents be sent to a concentration camp without at least trying to free them. In a daze, I picked up the file again, marched towards Mueller's office, and knocked on the door. I waited for the usual "Herein" and opened the door with a smile on my face. "Good morning, Herr Mueller, I have this file for you."

He seemed to be in a good mood. "Good morning, my child. Just leave it on that corner table."

"And how are things with you today, Herr Mueller? Christmas is not far away, you know." I deliberately used the more informal "Herr" rather than his official rank.

"Everything is fine, child," he said, looking pleased with my high spirits.

I turned towards the door, paused, and turned around again. "Oh! I almost forgot. May I talk to you for a moment, please?"

"Certainly. Sit down, Fräulein Olga, and tell me."

I sat down and began my story. I reminded him that I had been living in Brussels with an aunt of mine before the war. He nodded encouragingly. One day, I continued, my aunt had fallen sick and had taken to her bed with pneumonia. As her condition worsened, I had noticed that she could hardly breathe, and this had scared me. I had lost my head and run to seek help from a neighbour. The first I had approached, a woman who knew me, had practically slammed the door in my face with insults, saying, "Why don't you dirty Germans go back to Germany?" In desperation, I had called on some other neighbours, a middle-aged couple who lived upstairs above our apartment. They were most responsive and very kind; they came to my rescue, saw my aunt, and immediately called for an ambulance. My aunt recovered. She died a couple of years later of a heart attack, but always maintained that this couple, by their prompt intervention, had saved her life at that earlier time.

At this point I paused to watch Mueller's expression. He was listening to me attentively with his eyebrows raised, looking puzzled. I took a breath and continued. "Yesterday a woman who lives next door to that couple told me they were taken away to Malines a few days ago."

At the word "Malines", Mueller's whole countenance underwent an instant transformation. He stared at me with a hardened and ugly face and exclaimed, "Then they must be Jews!" I calmly proceeded with my fiction. I shrugged and said I guessed they must be Jews. But I owed them a debt, and that was why I hoped to obtain their release. So that he should not misinterpret me, I assured him that Jews in general were not my friends—far from it. I considered the mass of them as vermin that had to be destroyed. "But there are always exceptions everywhere, nicht wahr, Herr Mueller?"

He was still speechless. I said I knew him as a man of honour, straightforward and compassionate, whom I admired and respected; and that is why I had felt sure he would understand the reason for such an unusual request. I laid it on thickly and was gratified to note that my flattery did have some effect, for his features softened slightly; but his words were still harsh: "Fräulein Olga! What you are asking is insane! Whatever those damned Jews did for you and your aunt was expected of them! You do not owe them any debt. No one does."

I somehow hid my rage at these remarks behind a mask of indifference, though I could have strangled the beast then. At that moment someone knocked on the door and a Gestapo officer from another section walked in. Mueller dismissed me with a short wave of the hand, and offered a seat to the new visitor. I had lost.

But when I reached the door, he called me back. He was doodling on a scrap of paper with a pen as if lost in thought. Without raising his head, he muttered aloud, "I think I will save that Jew's skin. We can use him as an informer to catch other Jews." He removed a blank pass from his desk drawer and asked for the Jew's name. I spelled out Tobias Moszkiewiez for him, and he signed the pass and stamped it with the Gestapo seal.

Handing the document to me, he said, "Here. You may pick up the Jew, but you had better have one of our men go with you." I thanked him kindly, glanced at the pass, and saw that it was for one person only. In a matter-of-fact voice I asked, "And the woman?"

His reply shattered my hopes utterly. "We don't need the woman. Women and children are a nuisance; they get in the way. Sorry."

The other visitor had remained seated, silent and unconcerned. For some reason, his image remained engraved in my mind as I returned to my desk with a heavy heart, ready to give up my efforts.

The mere idea of my father acting as a traitor made me shudder, for I knew perfectly well that he would have spat in my face and disowned me as his daughter had I dared to hint, however remotely, that he could buy his freedom in such an exchange. I knew, too, that even if he were freed, he would never have left my mother behind.

I was utterly dejected that evening by the time I returned to my room at the Salvation Army. I sat on my bed and tore up the useless pass. My carefully-thought-out plan had depended on both my parents being released together. It had also required that a Resistance member, dressed as a German soldier, pick them up at Malines, pass in hand; from there they were to be taken straight to our maquis and sent to England via Spain or Normandy through one of the network escape routes. I myself had planned to vanish from the Gestapo immediately afterwards and join a maquis in France. Franz, of course, would have had to be warned so that he too could disappear. Now the whole scheme had collapsed, and I had no other plots with which to replace it.

Until the age of twenty-one I had lived at home; it was an anchor that had given me a measure of security. My marriage had lasted a little over one week. Now I had to face the fact that I was completely alone, essentially without any money, a Jewish girl in a Nazi-occupied city. What sustained me and strengthened my will to survive, then and later, was my fierce hatred of the Nazis and my hope that I would eventually see them lose the war and pay for their heinous crimes. I wanted to live, if only to be able one day to expose their cruelties to the world.

A week after I had spoken to Mueller, I passed him in the hall outside our office. He stopped me. "Fräulein Olga! What about the Jew you were supposed to bring in?"

I replied that it had completely slipped my mind to tell him that I had seen the Jew Tobias, but that when I had told him he would be working for us when freed, he had had the gall to refuse, mumbling something about the Germans doing their own dirty work, or words to that effect. As if dismissing the whole episode from my mind, I exclaimed, "Disgusting! You were right, Herr Mueller, all these Jews are the same. They are not worth bothering about. That will be a lesson to me!"

Mueller beamed. "You are very young, but you will learn," he said, and walked away.

And I did learn. Twice a month, a transport train manned by SS guards pulled in to the Malines railroad station to load its cattle wagons to capacity with Jewish civilians, men, women, and children, before starting its long trip across Germany to the remote death camps. There the train disgorged its human cargo, some of whom died during the trip. However, in the four months from December 1942 to April 1943, not a single train reached Malines, because the tracks were systematically bombed by the Allied air forces, disrupting the enemy's railroad traffic.

Finally, on April 20, a transport train arrived at Malines and picked up all the detainees, including my parents. While still in Belgium, the same train was held up by a well-armed Belgian Resistance group intent on freeing as many deportees as possible. But those prisoners able to jump off the train were machine-gunned by the SS guards, and only a few escaped alive. The majority, including my parents, could not break through the wagon doors. That train, remembered as Transport Number 20, was the last one to leave Malines for the death camps. My parents perished in the gas chambers, murdered by the Nazis together with the six million other victims.

About a month after I had last seen Estournier, I found irrefutable proof of his guilt by sheer coincidence. I was filing some documents at the Gestapo office when my eyes caught his name, signed at the bottom of a letter written presumably in his own hand. It was addressed to the chief of the Gestapo and said, in substance, that as a conscientious citizen, he had deemed it his duty to report the family of Jews who were hiding on the first floor of the house in which he lived. They were M. and Mme Moszkiewiez and their daughter Hélène. He gave our address but did not mention the standard reward, probably having decided that appropriating my father's cache of valuables would be reward enough.

I showed the letter to Franz, intending to remove it and keep it as evidence for after the war. He argued that it would be too risky to remove a document that Schwenke had personally seen. He might for some reason wish to see it again. He also pointed out that it might be years before it could be produced as evidence in a court of law.

These were valid arguments, so I asked what we were going to do about the informer. We contemplated his summary execution, but we both agreed that a painless death was too good for him. He should be made to suffer, and know why. I wondered if my father might one day settle with him, if he did return. We finally decided that Estournier would be allowed to live, but at a heavy price. At irregular intervals Franz, Jean, and I took turns phoning him in the middle of the night, to remind him in rough language that his day of reckoning was near and would arrive when he least expected it. We ensured that he lived in a state of constant fear, until his painful death of a heart attack soon after the Liberation.

Helene's parents in 1918. M. and Mme Moszkiewiez were sent to Germany on the last train bound for the concentration camps on April 20, 1943.

Helene (on the left) with her older sister, Lily, in the early 1920s.

Helene, aged five years, with Lily, aged ten.

Helene with Yvonne, one of her closest friends during their schooldays.

453 avenue Louise as it appears today, a quiet apartment building in Brussels. Helene worked on the eighth floor of the building during the time it served as the Brussels headquarters for the Gestapo.

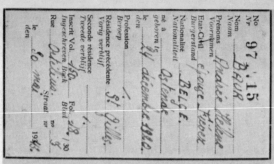

Helene's "fake authentic" identity paper, issued May 30, 1942, described her as Andrée Fiévez, the wife of a Belgian prisoner of war.

EN PLEIN JOUR,
LE 20 JANVIER 1943
CET IMMEUBLE, REPAIRE DE LA GESTAPO
DURANT LA GUERRE 1940-1945, A SUBI
LE FEU VENGEUR DES CANONS DE L'AVION DU

CAPITAINE BARON JEAN-MICHEL
DE SELYS LONGCHAMPS.

DU 1ER REGIMENT DE GUIDES
FLYING OFFICER A LA ROYAL AIR FORCE

This plaque on the former Gestapo building, avenue Louise, commemorates the air raid by a Belgian officer that killed a number of high-ranking Nazi officers on January 20, 1943.

Helene's first husband, Albert, to whom she was married for a week before he was detained by the Nazis. He later died in Auschwitz.

46 rue Léon de Lantsheere,
Brussels, where Helene
lived under an assumed
name for most of the war.

Helene and Albert, her
second-husband-to-be,
in uniform, with their
dachshund, Lottie, 1945.
Shortly after Albert's
return from a mission in
Germany, Helene and he
were married and they
emigrated to Canada.

By this

Certificate of Service

I record my appreciation of the aid rendered by

Mademoiselle *Helene Moszkiewiez*

as a volunteer in the service of the United Nations
for the great cause of Freedom.

B. L. Montgomery

Field Marshal
Commander-in-Chief, 21st Army Group

Date 8th April 1946
Serial No. B/0755

The citation awarded by the British to Helene
for her resistance work.

Helene in 1946.

9

Foiling the Foe

Until this time the Salvation Army had kindly provided me with
temporary accommodation and a job. Now it was urgent that I find a
safe and inexpensive place of my own, as well as a better-paying
position. Tips and advice from friends helped me secure both at about
the same time, under my new name as Andrée Fiévez, wife of a
Belgian prisoner of war.

I moved into a tiny furnished room on the first floor—which was
also the top floor—of a diminutive brick house on rue Léon de Lantsheere. This was a sleepy back street, and many of the houses on it,
like my new home, had been built around the turn of the century.
The only modern building on the street was the Clinique de Linthout,
a large structure housing a private mental hospital, directly across
from my room. The area was a discreet neighbourhood of retired
officials, widows, and petits bourgeois, perfectly suited to my needs for
privacy and concealment. My landlady, Mme de Bruyn, was a homely-
looking working widow with a heart of gold, and she had no other
lodgers. As she was a timid soul, she was only too glad to have some
company, as well as the extra income.

A few days after I had moved in, I found a new position, thanks to
the help of an old friend of the family named Josef Neuberg. Descended from a long line of German Jews and married to a German

Gentile, he had come to Belgium in the early 1930s, and at that time ran an insurance agency.

Herr Neuberg was in his sixties and retired when he and his wife met my parents. They had no children. He survived the German occupation under the protection of a special Gestapo permit issued to Jews who had married Gentiles before 1933, although his wife, who was much younger than him, later died during the war. By the time my parents were deported, the Neubergs were close friends of the family; they were very fond of me. Neuberg had influential friends, particularly in financial circles. When he heard about my parents' arrest and my own dire straits, he went out of his way to help me. He had learned through a banker friend that Baroness de Herrandt needed a children's governess; accordingly he sent me there with a fake testimonial stating that I, as Andrée Fiévez, had worked for his family in that capacity. The baroness did not check my credentials any further.

In addition to the baron and his wife, the household included three children, aged two, six, and eight years, the cook, and a chambermaid, a domestic staff considerably reduced on account of the war. My new employers and I agreed from the beginning that I would not actually live in the house, and that I would be allowed two half-days off each week, to attend to my own affairs. During these afternoons, of course, I was employed at Gestapo headquarters.

Franz was not at all pleased with my new job. He had hoped that I would reconsider his offer to work full-time with him in the Gestapo office, but I continued to remind him of my ignorance of written German and insisted that by remaining an unpaid part-time volunteer, I could enjoy greater freedom of movement. At this he went so far as to hint, albeit obliquely, that my very independence increased the possibility of my arrest. I did not appreciate the hint, and I realize in retrospect that it may well have been a veiled threat. At the time it seemed to me that Franz was beginning to assume some Gestapo tactics and behaviour patterns as his own. My experiences of the last few months had taught me that survival in this deadly game of secret warfare meant forestalling the moves of friend and foe alike. I assured Franz that he need not worry about me; I took his arm in mine, comrade fashion, and looked him straight in the eye: "If they ever arrest me, my dear, you may be sure that they will also arrest you. Don't forget that we are in this together, for better or for worse."

After that he kept his peace. I gave him my new address but made it very clear that he was not to call there except in an emergency, and never, ever, in uniform. My new home had no telephone.

My new position with the Herrandts proved satisfactory to the family and to me. Most important, I liked the children and they liked me. When I had been there for about three months, Baron de Herrandt called the household together and informed us that as of that day he was hiding from the Germans. He was pale as he announced calmly that in fact he expected a visit from the Gestapo at any time. When they came, we were to tell them that he had gone away. He asked the cook in particular—she was a Walloon who made no secret of her hatred of the Germans—to be on the look-out for them from her basement kitchen. From that window she stood eye-level with the pavement in front of the house, and so could see out without being seen. When the servants had been dismissed I lingered behind with the baron and casually asked him how he knew the Germans were after him. He admitted that he had twice received a summons to report for work to Germany, but he had ignored them, and intended to continue doing so. I nodded approvingly. I had no way of knowing at the time that he was himself involved in the Belgian Resistance. Only years after the war did I discover the connection.

The Boches did call a week later. Cook saw the blue Gestapo car pull up in front of the house and immediately sounded the alarm. The blue cars were used exclusively by Gestapo subsections, and the use of green cars was reserved for use of the avenue Louise headquarters. This slight distinction proved to be an invaluable piece of information to me. When the doorbell rang, I shortly ordered Cook back to her kitchen and the maid to her room. Then I told the baron to hide in the tool shed at the back of the yard. The baroness stood transfixed, gaping at me in the front hall. "Please, Madame, don't show yourself. I will handle this. Hurry!" The bell rang a second time, more insistently than before, and I went to answer the door.

Before either of the callers could open his mouth, I sharply demanded of them in German what they were doing there. They had come for Baron de Herrandt, they said, clearly startled to hear me speak German. They recovered sufficiently to request my papers and to ask what *I* was doing there. I abruptly produced my Gestapo pass. I was there on a special mission from headquarters, I told them in a low voice, and was handling the matter personally. They handed my pass back to me with great respect and apologized very meekly. I crisply demanded their papers in turn, pretended to peruse them, finally nodded approval, and bade them good evening. They clicked their heels smartly, saluted, and were gone. I closed the door behind me.

The baroness had not obeyed my injunction to hide. She had remained on the landing, leaning over the banister, and from that vantage point had seen and heard everything. I ascended several stairs towards her. "Madame, you were most unwise not to obey me when I asked you."

She stared at me with big black eyes and said quietly, "I did not know you spoke German, Madame Andrée. And you seemed to have considerable influence over those soldiers." She quietly beckoned me to follow her to the parlour, closed the door behind us, and asked me to sit down. Gravely she said she was most grateful to me, and she was deeply thankful for my timely intervention. "But," she said, "quite frankly, I am confused." She asked if it was true that my husband was a Belgian prisoner of war, as I had told her. I guessed what was on her mind, and answered quickly that I was certainly not German, but had been raised in Luxembourg, where I had learned to speak the language. "You must trust me," I said. "Unfortunately that is all I can tell you." She looked genuinely relieved and said she believed me, but wanted to know what document I had shown our callers. I repeated that I was not at liberty to say more, and advised her to forget the whole incident. And her husband, I added, should remain hidden for another hour or so, as the Gestapo could well return. If they did not call again within that time, she could assume that he was safe.

She wasted no time in telling her husband about me when he later emerged from his hiding-place. He invited me to his study and thanked me profusely for "saving his life", and shook my hand vigorously. He did not ask further questions himself.

The Boches did not call again, and my employers never mentioned the incident again. A few days later Mme de Herrandt tactfully suggested that I take off two full days a week in future, with no change in my salary. She said that the maid could look after the children during those days. We never discussed the arrangement any further and I was grateful for her discretion.

During my first months at the Gestapo, I concentrated on acquainting myself with office routines and moulding myself as a quiet employee. When I was more secure and the opportunity arose, I would do what I could to help the unfortunate victims of the Gestapo.

One of my daily chores was the sorting of various lists of hundreds of names and addresses, and classifying them by district and alphabetical order. The names were those of men to be impressed for forced labour in Germany, and they were to receive, or had already received, the dreaded summons. A few of these were usually earmarked for arrest, the ones who had failed to respond to the summons. Franz was supposed to forewarn these "delinquents" at his discretion, but I noticed that he gave them a low priority on his list of clandestine tasks.

While I was going through one of these lists one day, my eye was caught by an aristocratic name that seemed familiar. When I saw it repeated twice further, with different initials and with the title omitted, I was sure the names were those of the two sons of the Count de Bontour, so I asked Franz for permission to warn these people, claiming they were personal friends. That evening I called at the count's apartment.

The count himself was an elderly widower of considerable charm, and the uncle of Baroness de Herrandt. Although he owned a villa in the aristocratic suburb of Uccle, he preferred to live in his Brussels apartment on the more fashionable avenue des Nations, with his two sons and his servant. Occasionally he would drop in at the Herrandts' for tea or luncheon. Whenever he saw me, he would stop for a friendly chat, lightly addressing me as his ray of sunshine. As his appearances at the house increased over the months I gradually realized, as did the baroness, from stray compliments and a discreet hint or two, that he came principally to see me.

In the course of conversation over lunch one day, he mentioned his small villa in Uccle, and invited me to visit him there for tea some time. Ever curious and always interested in an extra meal, I accepted his invitation within the next weeks.

His "small" villa seemed more like a sumptuous mansion to me. The count watched me with special interest while I readily gorged myself on the fine cakes and pastries his cook had prepared. He must have guessed that I did not often eat a good meal. With great tact he instructed his servant to prepare a box of treats for me to take home later. Then he showed me around his property: spacious rooms, many of them panelled in oak; oil paintings on the walls; waxed parquet floors shining like mirrors partly covered in Persian rugs; Louis XV furnishings; expensive objets d'art; in short, the trappings of wealth and privilege wherever I looked. At the end of our tour, he looked at me steadily and asked, "How do you like ma petite villa?"

I honestly replied that I found it truly splendid, and not at all small.

"If you wish, Madame Andrée, it can be all yours."

"How do you mean, mine?"

He smiled. "I mean I would give it to you as a present; it would be transferred to your name. I will confess to you that I am very lonely; I need companionship. I like you, and ask you to be my companion. I would not be very demanding—not at my age, you understand. Just an occasional visit. A girl like you is not meant to be a governess. I rather fancy you would make a delightful hostess in this villa."

I listened, astonished, and rather flattered by the grand offer. Though he was charming and evidently generous, I saw him only as an old man and a fatherly, or even grandfatherly, friend. I certainly could not imagine him as my lover, nor myself as his mistress. His gallantry and the hopefulness in his expression impressed me. I did not want to offend him by too abrupt a refusal. "Your offer is very generous, Monsieur de Bontour, but I cherish my independence . . ."

He interrupted me gently. "Excuse me, Madame Andrée, but I can assure you that you would be entirely free, apart from my occasional visits. I would place my servants, my chauffeur, and my car at your disposal at all times. Rest assured that your time would be your own . . . What do you say?"

I had to remind myself that I was not living in a fairy tale. I promised again to think it over, and give him an answer in a few days. He looked pleased by this. "By all means, Madame Andrée. Whenever you are ready."

A few days later, he called when the baroness was out. After tea I asked him into the nursery. Though I had no intention of accepting his offer at that moment, I had thought about it carefully, for I knew the count's villa would make an ideal hide-out if I ever needed one in a hurry. I gave him an ambiguous answer. I told him how much I appreciated his proposal, that I was giving it serious thought and might well accept it a little later, but must decline it for the time being, as I needed all my free time just then. "I would like to ask for a rain check, if you would agree," I said. His pride was preserved: he smiled and readily agreed.

When I showed up at his apartment that evening, he did not look overly surprised. He must have thought that I was calling to give him a favourable answer to his proposal. He led me into the parlour, and I went straight to the point. "Monsieur de Bontour, I have come to warn you that your sons are in imminent danger of being arrested by the Gestapo. It appears that they did not answer the Nazis' summons, and they will be sent to Germany for forced labour or to a concentration camp if they refuse."

The count looked completely bewildered for only a few moments before he started asking questions. "But, my dear girl, how do you know that?"

"Through a friend."

"What friend? Do I know him?"

"I am sorry, I cannot tell you any more; but it is one-hundred-percent reliable. You can take my word for it." He looked at me carefully.

"If I were you," I added, "I would leave this apartment right away, with your sons. Your servant could stay. If and when the Gestapo calls, she can tell them you went away for an indefinite length of time."

The count, who had always impressed me as a shrewd man of the world, gazed at me in silence. He must have guessed by then that I was somehow involved in underground work. But with his customary tact, he said only, "Madame Andrée, I find you intriguing. I cannot make you out." I smiled and shrugged my shoulders, and apologized that I had to leave so soon. He thanked me again as he showed me to the door.

The next day he and his two sons left the apartment, leaving their servant in charge. When the count phoned later that same week, his servant told him that the Gestapo had indeed called and she had told them she did not know how long they would be away. The grateful count invited me again to his villa, this time for a formal dinner of thanks, but he never again alluded to his original proposal.

A secret agent who has successfully penetrated enemy forces must exercise a number of virtues, perhaps the principal of which is infinite patience. Obviously this was never one of my stronger traits. Franz often rebuked me for being too impulsive in various situations, but sometimes my impatience and spontaneous reactions, coupled with an innate presence of mind, saved lives, including my own.

One morning in 1943 I made my usual appearance at the office and found that Franz was out and had left no message. I tried to look useful by tidying his desk and filing away some papers, and while I was thus engaged, Mueller burst in, scowling. "Where is Leutnant Boehler?" he demanded. I said I had no idea, but supposed he would be in at any moment. Still agitated, he carried on, pacing up and down the room as he talked. "I have an urgent job for him as soon as he comes in. There are too many damned Jews hiding in this city. We have to root them out, fast. I don't care whether they're Belgian or not. A Jew is a Jew."

At this time Queen Elizabeth of Belgium, having learned that more Belgian Jews—including my husband Albert—had been deported despite her earlier protest, had appealed to the German high command for their protection a second time. Once again she had received assurances that her request would be respected, and once again a few token Belgian Jews had been released from the Malines transit camp. This gesture of appeasement infuriated Mueller. The Gestapo was authorized to override any agreement made by other authorities, German or not, concerning "the Jewish problem"—excepting, of course, any made by the SS. So under Mueller's command, the Gestapo persevered in its relentless persecution of Jews, of whatever age, sex, or nationality.

I made appropriate noises as Mueller ranted on that morning. "I have just received a list of Belgian Jews. I want them arrested right away. And I want Leutnant Boehler to handle this." He suddenly stopped in his tracks, as if struck by an idea. "Since you are here, Fräulein Olga, you may as well take down the following notice for translation into French. As soon as it is ready, bring it to my office, and I will have it typed. I will give you that list for Boehler later." He dictated, and I transcribed the following notice, translating it directly. If my memory is inaccurate, the original can doubtless be found in the archives of Brussels.

"Avis à la Population. [To the general public.] The population is hereby reminded that any person found harbouring Jews without immediately reporting them to the German authorities is punishable by prison, deportation, and confiscation of personal property. Signed, Mueller, Chief of Gestapo, Brussels."

Having finished, I took the proclamation to Mueller's office. He was not there and I seized my opportunity with only the slightest hesitation. If I could lay my hands on the master list of Belgian Jews, I could copy their addresses and possibly forewarn the intended victims in time to give them a chance to escape. Once the list was officially in Franz's hands or mine, the scheme would be much more difficult, as its execution would be traced to our office. To my great good fortune the infamous list was in full view on Mueller's desk. I rapidly scribbled the addresses on a piece of scrap paper as fast as I could, skipping the names for the sake of speed. I had taken down about thirty when I heard approaching footsteps. When Schwenke opened the door a moment later, I was conspicuously holding the translation in my hand. My list was thrust into my blouse.

Schwenke raised his eyebrows quizzically and asked me what I was doing there all alone. Entry to that office was strictly forbidden when neither the colonel nor the captain was there. I showed him my translation, answering truthfully that Oberst Mueller had ordered me to take it to his office as soon as it was ready. He nodded, satisfied, and began to talk as he sat at his own desk. "We have just arrested two spies and taken them to the cellar, and they'll certainly talk there! Oberst Mueller is interrogating them himself, so he may be away for quite a while. You needn't wait for him. Go back to your office."

The word "cellar" had frightful connotations at the Gestapo. It was a torture chamber worthy of the Inquisition. While walking through the downstairs hall towards the elevator, one could often hear the agonizing shrieks from below. On one occasion in my earlier days there, I had reacted very foolishly, and it could have cost me my life. Mueller had asked me to fetch one of the guard officers to his office, and along the way I had happened to pass by the head of the stairs leading to the cellar. I heard loud screams so heart-rending that I had lost my head and impulsively run down towards their source.

The door to the room was open and inside were two torturers, stripped to the waist, whipping a man who lay chained to what looked like a butcher block. His swollen body had been beaten to a pulp, a mass of deep gash-like welts and bleeding sores. When the brutes saw me, they stopped in astonishment. One of them demanded what the hell I was doing there. I snapped that the man's cries could be heard upstairs and asked, foolishly, what was their point in beating him to death if he wouldn't talk?

At that moment an officer had appeared at the doorway and asked me to explain my presence there. He listened to the torturers, then reprimanded me sternly. "You have no business here! It's against the rules! Wait a minute. I know you. Don't you work on the eighth floor?" I mumbled some feeble apology, but he still frowned and said that he would report me to the chief.

Mueller was equally annoyed with me. I listened to his lecture on disobedience and offered my weak heart as an excuse. I promised never again to interfere with departments that did not concern me and looked as sincere and contrite as I could. Mueller relented a little, repeated that there was a war on, and pointed out that I might not realize that the enemy did the same to our spies when they caught them. I knew he was lying but said nothing.

Franz was incensed when I admitted what I had done. To discourage further blunders, he made me get up at five o'clock one morning to come with him to avenue Louise, a prudent distance away from the

Gestapo building. At half past five, five plain wooden boxes—evidently coffins—were hauled out the front door and loaded onto a truck. "This happens every day," Franz told me. "They are prisoners who were tortured to death, or shot. If you do not watch yourself more carefully in future, you could easily end up in one of those boxes."

When I left Schwenke's office that day and returned to my own, I felt I had thirty human souls hidden on my person. I decided to leave early, intending to alert the marked victims without delay, but I needed help. I knew Jean was away on an assignment. Before leaving he had given me a list of phone numbers of other Resistance members who were to assist me if I needed help. I phoned the contacts but only one was available.

Louis's help was invaluable. I discovered not only that the addresses I had jotted down ranged widely all over greater Brussels, but that to obtain the phone number for each address, we had to know the names of the residents. Fortunately one of Louis's friends was an official at city hall with access to a cross-referenced register of names by domiciles. Louis also had the use of a car. We reached city hall before closing time and collected the information. Then we double-checked the addresses in the telephone directory at Louis's apartment and began our phone calls. Pretentiously Louis and I dubbed our job "Operation Alert" for the speed of its conception and blitz-like execution, all within less than twelve hours.

Little did I guess until that point what a thankless job I had undertaken. It was nearly impossible to persuade someone to whom I was only a strange voice on the telephone that he or she was about to be arrested by the Gestapo. There was of course no way that that person could be sure that Louis or I was not a prankster, a nut, or a burglar setting a trap. More often than not I met with suspicion, disbelief, or even rebuff. Our most difficult calls were those answered by some maid reluctant to disturb her employers for an anonymous caller. We used entreaties, and even threats, to directly contact every individual on the list. My sense of urgency, compounded with frustration, made the job very strenuous indeed.

After three solid hours of the exercise, I was all in; but we were not finished. Several addresses with no listed phone numbers remained, and these would require a personal visit. Without Louis's car further efforts to contact these people would have been hopeless. As it was, we did not complete our house calls until well after midnight. Had I not had my Gestapo pass with me in case we were stopped by a patrol, we might have had to abandon our efforts earlier.

For some reason I remember our last call very clearly. Our initial reception was openly hostile. A gaunt, bald man of about fifty sleepily opened the door. When I explained the reason for our late visit, he did not seem much interested. He was more curious to know who we were and why we were out at such an hour. His wife, who had been listening from the stairs, was more receptive. "What if they're telling the truth?" she asked her husband. Louis showed them his old Resistance card from the beginning of the war. In 1943 they were discarded, as too dangerous to carry, and replaced by verbal codes and passwords. The man consulted with his wife and finally decided to follow our advice; he immediately phoned a Gentile friend to arrange for temporary lodging. Only then did he remember to thank us and apologize for his earlier abruptness. I know that he was one of those who successfully eluded the Gestapo.

We had done all we could. I collapsed into bed around two in the morning, completely drained. When I told Franz what I had done, he said I had saved him some work, since he had intended to do the same thing but could not possibly have warned more than a limited number for fear of arousing suspicion. Meanwhile, he had passed the list, duly tabulated by districts, to the section responsible for executing the orders.

When the Gestapo had called to make their arrests at the listed residences, they returned it to Franz with a report of those arrested and those that could not be found at home. He told me that all but seven had been away when the Gestapo called. Most of the people Louis and I had called, then, must have heeded the warning after all, which gave me a great sense of relief and satisfaction. The full list had totalled some seventy-five names, almost all of them well-to-do Belgian Jews, some of them prominent businessmen or professionals who had remained in Brussels. As late as 1943, many of these, some with roots in Belgium going back several generations, were unaware of, or still unwilling to believe, the genocidal policies of the Nazi dictatorship. Many paid for their complacency with their lives.

On another afternoon, I arrived at the Gestapo office a little earlier than usual. Franz had gone out for lunch and was not expected back for an hour or so. I could hear Mueller screaming at someone next door, his harsh voice easily piercing the walls. I was wondering what was happening when he burst into my office and abruptly beckoned to me to follow him. He wanted me to do some interpreting for him.

A red-haired woman of about thirty stood in his office, facing his desk. I could tell at a glance that she was Jewish. Mueller sat down at his desk and, turning to me, said bluntly, "I cannot get anything out of this damned Jewess. Ask her where her husband and children are, and tell her that if she does not tell us the truth, she will be punished and deported."

I translated the message, trying to look as fierce as possible. Frightened though the woman obviously was, she repeated only the same negative answers in a strong Yiddish accent. I admired her determination to protect her family although I doubted very much that they could be saved. A man alone on the run could sometimes avoid detection by the Gestapo, but young children were not so easily kept quiet and out of sight. I felt I had to do something for her.

I told Mueller that she pretended not to know anything, and then suggested that I try a softer approach in a tête-à-tête conversation to dig the information out of her. He agreed. I took her to my office and had her sit down. I quietly listed the reasons why her children were in danger of being discovered and eventually sent to a concentration camp. I said I was willing to save her children, but that she would have to tell me where they were. She remained stone-faced, and I began to wonder if she really did have any children.

I tried again. "Listen, if you don't want to tell me, that's up to you. But I want you to understand; this is your only chance. I am in a position to place them where they would be safe, and remain alive."

She scrutinized my face with desperate eagerness and finally asked me softly, "Who are you? Are you German?"

I replied yes, and the chief's assistant.

"Then why would you want to save Jewish children?"

I had an answer ready, weak though it was. "To show you that we Germans are capable of humanitarian feelings. We are not all bad, you know."

Her unexpected response caught me off guard. "Aren't you afraid that I might report what you've just told me to your chief?"

Given her position, I considered the question a purely vicious and unwarranted threat. Perhaps she was just testing me further. Scornfully I retorted, "You fool! Do you really believe that your word as a Jewess would stand a chance against mine, a German? Why, I could have you destroyed with one word!"

She was not easily flustered, but asked again why I would want to save her children. I was relieved to note that she at least admitted to having children.

"Because I like children," I replied, "and do not believe that they should be harmed. Listen, we haven't much time. Do you, or do you not, want them to stay alive?" I waited as she considered. In the end she asked me where I intended to take them. "To the Red Cross," I told her. "They will place them on a farm, out of danger." She finally disclosed that her children were with friends.

"Are these Jewish friends?"

"Yes."

"Then they are certainly not safe. They should be removed from there at once."

She gave a shrug of sad resignation and said, almost inaudibly, "What have I got to lose?" Meekly she gave me the address. I tried to instil some hope in her, by telling her that she could apply to the Red Cross after the war for their safe return. "Thank you," she whispered, her head lowered.

To the credulous chief I reported that I had been unable to make her talk, but that I felt sure that she did not know where her family was hiding. His profound disappointment was gratifying. The woman was taken away.

That same evening, I fetched the three children—one girl and two boys, the eldest of whom was nine—from their hide-out. I had no trouble persuading their hosts to hand them over when I suggested they come with me to the Red Cross headquarters only ten minutes' away. I left the three waifs in the care of the nurse on duty, and she promised to send them to one of their farms in the countryside.

Whether they were ever reunited with their parents, I never knew. But even if they were the only survivors of their family, three lives saved were better than none. Volumes would be required to record the humanitarian work of the International Red Cross both during and after the Second World War. There are thousands of such stories that will never be told.

10

Escape Routes

As the months went by, my presence at the Gestapo, twice a week, sometimes in the morning and sometimes in the afternoon, was accepted as a matter of course by the other inmates. I was just one of the many women—military and civilians—employed in the various sections and different floors of the building. I remember that week after week Franz kept me busy at his office going through masses of papers, which I had to sort out, classify, file away, or distribute to other sections. It was a routine and boring task, and whenever I complained to Franz, he promised that I would soon have an opportunity to prove myself in the field. Finally, in the spring of 1943, the break came, when a chance remark made by Schwenke during a casual conversation with Franz led me on a risky mission that took me much farther afield than most of my assignments.

Schwenke had casually alluded one day to a nest of spies operating from a private home on the chaussée de Louvain. When Franz had just as casually asked him why they had not yet been arrested, the captain had answered with a knowing wink that Mueller was biding his time, intending to capture the lot in one surprise raid within the next few days.

Franz repeated the disquieting conversation to me that evening when he called at my place. We now found it too dangerous to discuss such matters at the headquarters, especially as we had recently been moved to a larger office, beside the one shared by Mueller and Schwenke. We had pretended to be delighted with the new office, loudly praising it as a tremendous improvement, but actually we found the new arrangement stifling. A door now connected the two offices, so our neighbours could hear everything we said. As a result we had learned to communicate by signs or to simply avoid any comments that could arouse suspicion.

Franz had come to my place to discuss what we could do to prevent the arrest of the spies. Neither Franz nor Jean, nor anyone else in the local Resistance, apparently knew anything about them. We could only presume that they belonged to some other network. Franz did not know the number of the house on the chaussée de Louvain, and as the road is a long one, we were helpless to warn the victims. We reasoned that there ought to be a file somewhere on so important a group, and that its logical place would be in Mueller's office. Finding it, I was told, would be my job. Franz's plan was simple enough. We would wait until both officers had gone to the café for their morning break. Then I would sneak into their office through the connecting door to look for the file. There were a lot of ifs, but it was worth a try.

That morning we were at our office desks bright and early. Promptly at ten o'clock the two officers went out for their break, and five minutes later I was in their office, a document in my hand and the connecting door open in case Mueller unexpectedly reappeared. I began searching feverishly for the dossier through the piles of papers and files on both desks. After more than ten minutes' search I was about to give up, when I spied a binder marked "C/L" (for chaussée de Louvain) under a sheaf of reports. That was it! I swiftly found the address, memorized it, and replaced everything, ready to leave.

At that moment the door on the hall side opened and Schwenke walked in. I still held the decoy document in my hand, and I smoothly laid it on Mueller's desk as if I had just entered to do so. When Schwenke asked me what I was doing in the office, I indicated the sheet. He frowned at me. "Fräulein Olga, I believe I have told you before not to enter this office when there is no one else here."

In my most business-like tone I replied, "Sorry, Herr Schwenke, I knocked on the door before entering, but of course I should have waited for an answer instead of rushing in. I will remember next time."

He wagged his finger at me and let me pass. Suspicion did not really enter his mind; he viewed the episode as merely a matter of

German discipline. To my mind, however, the incident was a close call, and I resolved that he would not find me alone in that office a third time. Back in our office I blamed Franz for the near disaster and accused him of carelessness. His weak excuse was that he had been immersed in a report and had neglected to watch the hall.

Promptly after work, we set out to call on the spies at their hide-out. We asked Jean and one of his men to join us, and all four of us, including Franz, who drove, carried our revolvers for safety.

We found the house just as darkness was closing in. After cruising back and forth a few times to ensure that the place was not being watched by anyone else from the street, Franz parked some hundred feet short of the house. When we had watched it for about an hour more and seen no movement in or out, we decided to move. It was completely dark when Jean, his friend, and I walked to the door. Franz remained at the wheel, to keep watch along the street.

We rang the bell twice. No one answered. We rang again several times more and banged on the door with our fists until a rough-looking youth finally opened it a crack, peered at us suspiciously, and gruffly asked what we wanted. Jean replied that we were from the Resistance and had come to warn them of a Gestapo raid; but the youth would not admit us. Through the narrow opening, he insisted that we were making a mistake.

"Listen, we happen to know that you are in danger of being arrested," Jean insisted firmly, "and we only came to help you. But we can't talk in the street. Why not let us in?" He paused a moment and then abruptly forced the door open with a powerful kick.

We all slipped in quickly, closing the door behind us, to find ourselves confronted by a second tough character behind the doorman and two other men who stood on a landing at the top of the stairs, each pointing a sub-machine-gun at us. Jean repeated himself, assuring them that we were members of the Resistance ourselves and that they could trust us. The older man in the hall, apparently the leader, asked for our credentials. I carried only my fake German papers and Gestapo pass, and Jean, on principle, never carried any such incriminating identification.

Fortunately, Jean's friend still had his old Resistance card with his identification number. The leader took it and went to the phone to make a call. Evidently he received the information he had requested, for he hung up and said to the others, "They're on the level. We can talk." One of them seemed only half persuaded, and he asked what the man outside was doing. When I answered that he had been left there to keep watch, they finally invited us into the parlour. There they relaxed and opened up.

There were eight of them in hiding, part of an underground network operating in northern France. They had just arrived in Belgium on a special assignment when they learned that the rest of their group, including their radio operator, had been arrested in France. They were now stranded without alternate instructions and hoping for further orders, which did not seem to be forthcoming. By good fortune a friend had let them occupy the empty house.

Jean spoke for us. "I see only four of you here. Where are the others?" They were out, we were told, but could be reached at any time. "Fine, then contact them as soon as you can," Jean ordered. "Immediately after we leave, abandon this place, and do not return. I repeat, *do not return here under any circumstances.*"

"And where do we go from here?" asked one of them, looking nervous.

"I was coming to that," said Jean. He looked at his watch. "The time is now 1830 hours. At 2000 hours all eight of you will congregate at the Café du Coq, on the corner of rue St-Josse and the chaussée de Louvain. A covered German truck will stop a little further up the street, near the church. Get into the back as fast as you can, one at a time, without attracting any more attention than you have to. The driver will be wearing a Wehrmacht uniform but he'll be one of ours and will take you straight to our headquarters. They'll look after you there."

There were no further questions, so we shook hands all round, wished them luck, and departed.

Jean phoned his Resistance chief immediately afterwards to check on the eight men, their code names and numbers. Had there been the slightest doubt about their identities, we would have had to dispose of them. However, their stories cleared, and they were picked up and safely taken to the Namur maquis.

The maquis lay hidden deep in the Ardennes forest, some distance from Namur, a town in the Walloon sector of Belgium. It consisted of a system of underground dug-outs connected by tunnels that led to carefully concealed entrances in different clearings. The surrounding area was thoroughly mined as a protection against possible enemy forays. Any stranger admitted to the maquis was guided through a maze in the minefield by one of the men on sentry duty who was familiar with the trail. The dug-outs themselves had many purposes,

as meeting-places, sleeping quarters, offices, as well as storage rooms
for small arms, ammunition, German uniforms, and whatever else had
been garnered from enemies killed in ambush. Various vehicles were
distributed in the clearings, and even a small fleet of German trucks
was hidden under loads of hay or firewood at a nearby farm. Extra
reserves of arms and ammunition were carefully concealed on the
same farm. The farmer, an elderly man whose name I have forgotten,
was decorated after the war for the great risks he had taken in helping
the underground.

These headquarters willingly gave temporary hospitality to members of other groups in need of it, but they did not have the facilities
for a prolonged stay. After a week or so, therefore, the chief decided
that the eight maquisards had to be taken off their hands, and since
Franz had been the prime mover behind the operation, he was politely
instructed to organize an escape route for the men.

Franz requested certain items of equipment from the camp, including one of the Wehrmacht covered trucks, eight Wehrmacht soldiers'
uniforms, complete with documents; five bottles of Steinhäger; eight
German service rifles, with rounds of ammunition; and one uniform,
small size, of the Blitzmädchen, the women's auxiliary service.

This last item, he informed me, was for my use. This was the first I
had heard of my inclusion in the operation, so Franz briefed me. "We
will be heading for the Swiss border. I'll be driving, in my Gestapo
outfit. It's rather a long journey, so one of your jobs will be to keep
me from dozing off behind the wheel. You may also be useful, if
necessary, to distract the guards' or sentries' attention with some
friendly chat, or whatever other tricks will be necessary. Last but not
least, you'll be company." I was to be ready at noon the next day.

I reported sick to Mme de Herrandt and promised to be back to
work as soon as I felt better. For his part Franz always found plausible
excuses for his absences to satisfy Mueller. He could claim to be on
the trail of a spy, or a parachutist, or other suspicious character. Partly
because of his fluent knowledge of English and French, Mueller permitted him relatively free movement in his position.

On the following afternoon we drove straight to the Namur camp.
There we found the equipment ready, and the eight men waiting for
us. They had already donned their Wehrmacht uniforms and were
handed their rifles and some ammunition. None of the French boys
could speak a word of German so they were ordered to keep their
mouths shut, snore, or give unintelligible grunts attributable to drunk-
enness if addressed at any check-point during the trip. At first they

objected to the German schnapps we insisted they drink, and they promptly spat it out. They were essentially wine-drinkers and unaccustomed to the potent liquor. But they were told to gargle with the stuff and smear their faces with it to produce a credible reek. From time to time they were to repeat the dousing, to keep up a convincing appearance.

We all ate quickly and at last took our seats in the truck, each man holding his rifle. As a final touch, half-filled bottles of schnapps were placed around our passengers, in seemingly haphazard fashion. With me in my Blitzmädchen uniform, we started out a little after six o'clock that evening.

An hour later we crossed the French border with no trouble. The Wehrmacht sentries we met let us pass through as soon as they saw our officer in charge. Almost all personnel of the regular army, from the lowest private to the highest-ranking officers, feared and loathed the Gestapo, and this helped us considerably along our way.

After driving in the dark for several hours, we arrived at the old demarcation line. This line separated German-occupied France from unoccupied Vichy France, a distinction the Gestapo often ignored. But we were stopped at a fully manned check-point, where the officer in charge was exceptionally thorough. He examined our papers carefully and asked where we were going.

Franz said that we were heading for a particular village—the name of which I have forgotten—not far from the Swiss border. We had orders, he said, to capture several parachutists known to have landed in the neighbourhood, and now hiding. He had taken a small detachment of soldiers with him for the purpose, but they had scrounged some bottles of Steinhäger somewhere and were disgustingly drunk just now. This last information he added as if unconcerned. The officer glanced inside the truck and saw some soldiers snoring, others staring bleary-eyed at the bottles by their elbows. He shook his head in disapproval and grumbled "Schweinerei!" (Disgusting!), but the men were not his to rebuke.

He finally sent us on our way, and we drove off with a big sigh. That was our last major obstacle. I remember the rest of the night as one long, bumpy ride. We reached the Franco-Swiss border around midnight, at a point seldom patrolled by frontier guards. There our passengers disembarked, leaving their guns behind. Now they would have to find their way to the Swiss side on their own, along a narrow trail used occasionally by local peasants and their goats. It meandered through the hilly woods, leading deep into Swiss territory. By the time the Germans tightened their grip on France in subsequent months, the Goat Trail had become so popular as an escape route that Jerry had to place extra guards there with trained dogs, effectively closing another door to freedom.

Our eight men were provided with a map of the area, cutters for the inevitable barbed wire, and a length of rope. They were instructed to walk in single file in complete silence, linked together like mountaineers to keep anyone from straying. They also carried their French identity papers to show the Swiss authorities, who would otherwise return them to German-occupied France as German deserters.

We waited about half an hour after they had gone, listening for any warning noises, such as gunshots or barking dogs, that would indicate that the escape party had been detected. We heard nothing at all, and so assumed that everything had gone as planned. We filled the gas tank from the jerrycans we had brought with us and started for home. During the trip back, I had to prod Franz repeatedly to keep him from dozing off. The sun was rising as we crossed into Belgium. We arrived in Brussels in broad daylight after driving for some thirteen hours, with only two half-hour stops. Back in my flat at last about eight that morning, I dropped into a deep sleep as soon as I fell into bed.

Some months later we learned through a chance contact that our eight maquisards had safely crossed into Switzerland and been interned, then turned over to the Red Cross. From there they had managed to return to France, where they joined up with another maquis, for a second time. I heard no more of them. Perhaps some of them are alive today.

Not all the fugitives I knew were so lucky, as I am often reminded when I think of Rachel Goldman. I was at home one evening around ten o'clock and ready for bed when the doorbell rang, and someone knocked repeatedly on the door. Mme de Bruyn, my landlady, had already gone to bed herself. She must have been peering through her window, for she called me and came out on the landing in her nightshirt, visibly shaking. Only the Gestapo called at that time of night.

"Madame Andrée, it's the Boches! What would they want with us?"

They could only have come for me. With a constricted throat and sinking feeling, I descended the stairs to open the door, desperately trying to think of who could have betrayed me. Only Franz knew my address, but surely he would never have informed on me. Trembling, I admitted the two callers in the small front hall.

They were particularly tough-looking characters. One of them asked in broken French if there was a Jewish girl in the house. I answered in German that there was no Jewish girl on the premises, adding that I myself was German, and worked for the Gestapo, avenue Louise. This did not seem to impress them. The one who had spoken in French laconically asked for my papers. I told him they were in my room, and they followed me upstairs, aggressively shoving me from behind.

It was then that I suddenly remembered having seen a dark-haired girl with pronounced Jewish features entering the house two doors away from ours several days before. It was just possible that the Gestapo were actually looking for her, and had knocked on the wrong door. This possibility helped restore my self-assurance.

Poor Mme de Bruyn still stood on the landing, absolutely paralyzed with fear and not understanding a word of our exchange. In her long night-shirt and with the mass of hair-curlers framing her face, she resembled a chimpanzee. The Gestapo thugs burst into rude laughter at the sight and pushed by her. In my tiny room, I showed them my German identity card and Gestapo pass, knowing full well that if they had a description of me, they would disregard any documents and arrest me anyway. They seemed to accept them and looked around my room, obviously mystified, for Gestapo personnel in occupied areas invariably enjoyed the best available accommodation.

My furniture, however, consisted of a bed, a wardrobe, a small cast-iron heating stove, a gas burner, and a table and chair, with just enough elbow room for one small person. Gas for cooking was made available to consumers for only one hour at noon and for two hours between five and seven in the evening. As I seldom returned home before six o'clock, I had one hour of gas and one burner on which to cook, heat, or boil water. Also there was no hot running water in the house, so I had learned to wash with cold water from the sink on the landing.

"What are *you* doing in such shitty quarters?" one of the men asked in surprise.

I had a quick answer. I told them I was waiting for my fiancé, an officer at Gestapo headquarters, to move into his new apartment, which was why I had not installed a phone. They nodded curtly, but insisted on searching the entire house very thoroughly. Finally admitting that they might have the wrong address, they asked me where they could find a phone. I directed them to a café some distance away, hoping this would give me time to warn the girl next door. I was sure by that time that they were after her, and not me.

As soon as they had left, I told my worried landlady about the girl, and my intention to forewarn her. She begged me not to interfere, as I threw my coat on over my night-clothes. It was winter and bitterly cold outside as I ran over to the neighbouring house.

A middle-aged woman answered the door. She was a widow who lived all alone and she denied sheltering anyone. "Madame, please listen to me, I beg of you. The Gestapo may be here any minute, and you'll be arrested too if they find a Jewish girl hiding here." The stubborn woman continued her denials until the girl herself appeared on the upstairs landing in her night-shirt.

"I overheard the conversation. You're right. I am Jewish. So what do you want me to do? I have nowhere else to go."

I told her to grab her coat immediately and come with me. "And you, Madame," I told the woman, "tidy up her room. Make it look as if no one had been living in it recently. If the Boches smell a rat, they'll arrest you."

So Rachel Goldman spent the night with me, despite my landlady's terrified protests. Rachel's story was all too familiar. Two weeks earlier, while she was out shopping, her parents had been dragged from their home by the Gestapo, and deported. She could not return home and could think of nowhere else to go. Then she had remembered the address of a Gentile woman, an old friend of her mother's, to whom she appealed for shelter. That lady was the widow next door, and she had kindly agreed to take her in, but for a few weeks only, as she herself was short of food.

I called on her again the next day to pick up Rachel's few belongings, and she generously gave me several cans of food—"to help out," she said. These were most welcome, as my own rations were barely enough to sustain even one person. In fact I could not have survived on them myself, had I not also had a free noontime meal at the Herrandts' five days a week.

Mme de Bruyn was very kind-hearted, and she allowed Rachel to stay in her attic for a few days more until I could find a Resistance truck to take her to some relatives who lived on a farm in the country. Rachel had not dared to travel any further alone for fear of arrest, since she had no false identity papers. When she left, she promised to keep in touch with me, if she possibly could.

A few months later, I met the agent who had driven Rachel to the farm. He told me that he had returned there recently, and been told that the Gestapo had raided the village, looking for a couple of Jews in hiding. While making a routine check at the farm where Rachel and her relatives were staying, they had found them and taken all of them away. I never heard from her again, so I can only assume that she was one of those who did not survive the ordeals of the concentration camp.

The saddest part of the story is that the Gestapo never came back to our street. I have often wondered what would have happened to the girl if I had not tried to save her that night. Perhaps she would have survived the war and the Holocaust; but perhaps not, after all. The odds were certainly against her survival. At the time I did what I thought was the only thing I could do, and faced with the same situation today, I know I would act in exactly the same way.

11

Reckless Reactions

I do not intend to dwell on the discomforts, privations, and indignities of everyday life in Brussels during those years under the Nazi regime. I should explain, however, that the difficulties in my case were compounded. In addition to the constant worry of obtaining the barest necessities of life on my meagre income, and being broke most of the time, I had to be always on the alert as a part-time Gestapo spy, and especially a Jewish one. I never overcame my chronic terror of being recognized and hustled off to the dreaded cellars every time I set foot in the Gestapo building. The cumulative effect of such tensions weighing on my mind brought me dangerously near the breaking-point several times. The worst moments, however, were those when I was compelled to act out my hated role for the enemy to protect my cover. One such case was that of the heroic Belgian girl I saw being caught by the Gestapo.

I was on my way to work on avenue Louise one morning when I noticed a Gestapo car and an army truck parked in front of an elegant home on the same street. Two Gestapo thugs were roughly dragging out a young woman, still in her night-gown, while others busied themselves with loading several heavy boxes into the truck. Judging from their appearance, I guessed the boxes might have contained arms and ammo. I pitied the poor girl but forced myself to walk on.

I had expected to see Franz at the office, but, as happened so often those days, he was out. I generally disliked the idea of being alone there because I felt so exposed and unprotected. As time went on, I thought Franz seemed to show less and less concern for my safety or well-being. His attitude towards me now was consistently detached and business-like, a definite change from the days when we had been good friends and had gone out together for fun. Either he had changed greatly, I decided, or he was some kind of double personality. Once when I was completely broke, to the extent that I could not even afford to buy any food, I asked him if he could let me have some money. He said he was sorry, but he was broke himself, and complained that he had not received any funds from London. I was too proud to beg any further.

I started my usual filing duties. I could hear the raised voices of Mueller and a French-speaking woman next door. Suddenly Mueller burst into my office, evidently seeking Franz. When he saw me instead, he looked relieved.

"Ah! Fräulein Olga! I need an interpreter. Will you please come to my office?"

I immediately recognized the girl I had seen being manhandled on the street only an hour earlier. Despite her night-gown she stood erect and defiant in Mueller's office, a tall, beautiful girl with long golden hair, probably in her early twenties. Mueller sat down behind his desk. For my benefit he asked her, in German, to give me the names of her contacts and accomplices and to explain how she had obtained the arms. In answer she spat in his face. He wiped his cheek with his handkerchief while I silently applauded her. He calmly ordered me to translate his questions into French. When I did, she turned and spat derisively in my face.

Instinctively I slapped her, exclaiming, "No one spits in *my* face!" As soon as I had reacted, I felt terribly sorry. I understood her feelings only too well and shared them, but there was not a thing I could do to help her. I knew she was doomed, and from the look in her eyes she must have known it too. Mueller had her taken away. I shuddered at the thought of that healthy young body being tortured, then shot. She did not seem to me to be a woman who would eventually break down and talk. As they marched her away, she held her head high, singing "La Brabançonne", Belgium's national anthem, in a loud clear voice for all to hear. I may never know her name, but, dead or alive, she deserves the highest admiration and honour.

After this depressing episode, I was astonished to learn that Mueller had been deeply impressed by my reaction to the girl's spirit. He repeatedly praised me before other Gestapo personnel and in my presence, recounting the details of the scene as if I had acted with great courage. I suppose he had considered me a little girl incapable of decisive action, and the incident had completely amazed him. However much I personally regretted my action, Mueller's compliments certainly strengthened my cover.

Incidents like these alerted me to a potential problem as well. I was forced to recognize that I was stifling a tremendous amount of frustration. Sometimes I seemed to simply explode in the form of some daredevil gesture of defiance, which could have cost me dearly, as the following case will show.

Mueller mentioned to me one day that he expected an official visit of a VIP the following morning, some SS general or other, to avenue Louise headquarters. He asked me if I would like to be present, and, sensing that this might be a test of my loyalty, I eagerly accepted. "Of course, Herr Mueller, that would be a very great honour for me!"

He smiled and told me that I would have to wear a uniform, and he promised to find me one. The outfit he eventually found was not what I had expected. It was several sizes too large, so that the sleeves covered my hands and the skirt literally brushed my ankles. I was sure it made me look like a scarecrow, especially when someone else told me I looked much smaller and younger than usual in it.

The next morning, all eighth-floor personnel were precisely assembled in the hall. We stood at attention, awaiting review by the general and his retinue. The clerical staff had heard that some of the visitors had been entertained the previous night at a party that had ended in an orgy, not an unusual entertainment for the higher ranks, as I had discovered one evening. Franz and I had been working overtime at the office—actually collecting vital information for London—when I heard strange noises from next door. I was puzzled that Franz pretended not to hear anything. I knew that neither Mueller nor Schwenke normally stayed so late, but when I asked Franz about it, I was curtly told, "It's none of our business."

Dissatisfied, I decided to find out for myself. I knocked on the door, heard a slurred "Herein!" and opened it. Inside sat Mueller, his eyes bleary with lust and drink, holding a struggling, half-naked girl on his lap and trying to force drink down her throat. A second girl lay naked on the floor, crying, while she was raped by another officer. Two other men were in the middle of undressing and fondling a third weeping girl.

I was so shocked and disgusted that I involuntarily exclaimed, "Schweinerei!" Fortunately they were all so drunk that they did not seem to hear me. I angrily slammed the door shut and marched back to our office.

Outraged, I asked Franz if he knew what was going on in the next room. He answered with a shrug that it was nothing new. "Now and then," he said, "when these gentlemen are in their cups, they wait on the sidewalk in front of the building, and grab—or 'arrest'—any girl who passes at that moment. They take her to their office, force her to drink, and then rape her, everyone in turn. If they're satisfied, they let her go. Some of the girls are lucky to get out alive."

I stared at him. "They're just a bunch of common criminals!"

He smiled. "What are you going to do about it, Olga dear? Girls shouldn't be walking past Gestapo headquarters after dark." Both the remark and his tone of voice appalled me. I had not suspected this side of Franz.

At long last the brass arrived. The general, a middle-aged man looking full of his own importance, strutted before us. As he passed each rigid uniformed figure, he stopped briefly, raised his right arm from the elbow up, and barked, "Heil Hitler!" When he had received the same salute and answering bark, he moved on. With mechanical regularity the performance was repeated all along the line. He finally stood in front of me, raised his arm, and exclaimed, "Heil Hitler!" in a resounding voice.

I don't quite know what came over me, but I pertly answered in my small voice, "Grüss Gott!"—which, despite its literal translation, is no more innocuous a greeting than "Good day". All eyes swung to stare at me in the shattering silence that followed. The general looked nonplussed by my response, took a closer look at me, and hesitated for a fraction of a second, before repeating his salute somewhat louder. To return the correct greeting, I figured, would have been an admission of guilt. So I braced myself and said again, firmly, "Grüss Gott!" I explained with my most engaging little girl's smile, "Herr General, der Führer ist mein Gott, mein einziger Gott!" (The Führer is my God, my only God!) Still taken aback, the officer raised an eyebrow, pondered, smiled to himself, nodded, smiled again, and finally said, "Very good, my child, very good indeed!" Then, to humour such childish faith in the beloved leader, he looked squarely at me and bellowed, *"Grüss Gott!"* Immediately another officer in his party stepped forward and fervently crowed, "Grüss Gott!" and stepped back again smartly, like a toy soldier. The day was saved from disaster, but I was not spared the recriminations.

Mueller was the first to beckon me into his office afterwards. There he lectured me with a certain avuncular mien on the differences between "Heil Hitler" and "Grüss Gott"; the latter, he explained patiently, was something quite different. I listened politely and, with a sweet parting smile, wished him "Grüss Gott" as I left. He must have attributed my impertinence to mere childish mischief, for all he did was shake a finger at me, noting that my behaviour was "something I would expect from my young daughter".

Schwenke's reaction, however, was far more serious. He described the need for strict compliance with the rules regarding the "Heil Hitler" salute, and the dire consequences of any such breach of discipline in the future. When I rebutted him, quoting the general's approval, ending the interview with my "Grüss Gott", he dismissed me with a gesture of disgust. I knew he would pick on me at the next opportunity.

There were further criticisms at the office, where the secretary was also lying in wait for me. Her approach was more direct. "Fräulein Olga! I must say that in my opinion you disgraced us this morning! You behaved like an ill-mannered child. Not only that, but I believe you did it all on purpose, to draw attention to yourself."

My reply was in French—"J'vous emmerde tous!"—which, in polite English, would translate as "You can all go to hell."

She heard me but she could not understand my French, claiming that I spoke too rapidly for her. She sharply asked me to repeat in German what I had just said. Making for the door, I replied with a smile, "Oh! I simply said you were perhaps right," and left the room.

The strongest reprimand, however, came from Franz, who bluntly accused me of jeopardizing our whole cover with dangerous frivolities. He was right, of course, and I promised to be more cautious in future.

Meanwhile, the war dragged on, month after month, year after year. For anyone who has not lived under enemy oppression, it is very hard to understand the gloom and despondency that one feels from time to time when there is no end in sight. I knew, of course, that my lot was still preferable to that of those herded into the concentration camps. Nonetheless there were days when I was tired of the stealth, the precautions, the whole cloak-and-dagger style of life I had to lead, and cared about nothing. In such moods I was tempted to take wild chances. Owing to one such mood, I came to within a hair's breadth of disaster. And perhaps that same desperate mood is what saved me that time.

Many German hand-guns and ammunition that were stolen for use by the Resistance found their way to the maquis. These were wrapped in small parcels, easily carried by one individual, and passed from place to place by a relay system of delivery. Within the city, women members of the Resistance were often carriers of these dangerous parcels, as they were less likely to be searched than the men.

One sweltering summer day in 1943, Franz summoned me to his apartment and showed me a small valise containing three German service revolvers, three hand-grenades, and a box of ammunition, all carefully packed in straw to minimize rattling. The valise had been delivered to him a few hours earlier. He told me that I was to act as courier, delivering the valise to the Gare du Midi in downtown Brussels. His instructions were concise: "You will walk all the way. Do not ride any trolley-cars or other vehicles, under any circumstances. Once at the station, go to the waiting-room, and make sure it is not being policed by the Feldgendarmerie or the Gestapo. The latter are often in mufti, but they're easily recognizable.

"Look for a Wehrmacht soldier sitting on a bench facing the first wicket on your right. He'll have a valise that's absolutely identical to yours. It will contain women's clothing. The soldier is one of our own men, but do not talk to him. Just sit next to him and place your valise beside his. He is supposed to catch the 4:55 train to Namur. He will pick up your case and leave his. When he has gone, wait another fifteen minutes, then check your suitcase at the baggage office, and return here by the fastest means available. If you can find a taxi, take it. I'll pay for it."

He locked the valise and gave me the key, which hung on a thin chain. I was to wear it around my neck, the key hanging deep down the front of my blouse. The soldier would have a duplicate key.

I set off on foot. The heat was oppressive, the valise heavy for one of my size and weight, and my destination almost an hour's walk away. In those years the city of Brussels did not have a subway system like the Paris Métro or the London Underground. Instead a large fleet of trolley-cars, called tramcars, criss-crossed greater Brussels and its suburbs on rail tracks. During the war the trolley-cars were the old model, with open platforms front and rear, where passengers could stand if they did not wish to sit inside. Until the end of the war these and a few trolley-buses were the sole means of transportation for the bulk of the city's population. The Wehrmacht or Feldgendarmerie often stopped the cars at random check-points and ordered the passengers off to have their papers inspected, hoping to find Jews or escapees or to confiscate small arms. I rode on trolley-cars all the time but had never once met a road-block. As I panted along that afternoon I rationalized the temptation to myself: "Why should I have to avoid riding a tramcar today of all days? To hell with it! I'll take the chance!"

I hopped on a car bound for the Midi station. After about ten minutes the car came to a sudden halt, and a soldier stuck his head inside and shouted, "Alle aussteigen!" I was seized with panic and the absolute certainty that all was lost. Very slowly the feeling of panic subsided as I waited my turn. I knew then how one can risk everything in a final desperate gamble, and as I descended from the car, I was deadly calm.

The passengers obediently filed out and lined up on the sidewalk, waiting to be checked one at a time by a corporal on duty. If I were actually forced to open the case, I had decided to grab a hand-grenade from my valise, simultaneously removing the pin, throw it at the soldier's feet, and run. I risked being shot as I escaped, but I preferred that to torture or a concentration camp. Now that I had determined my next move, I was ready.

The corporal checked my Andrée Fiévez card, approved it, and handed it back to me. Glancing at the valise at my feet, he said casually, "Aufmachen." I pretended not to understand German. He pointed and repeated, "Die Valise aufmachen." I played dumb, made a gesture of incomprehension, and replied in French, "Comprends pas."

Behind me the other passengers were becoming impatient and muttering. One of them, a big burly fellow with a stentorian voice, yelled at me, "Don't you understand German? He says open your bag!"

I took this as my cue to turn around like a fury and pour out a torrent of abuse on the man. He responded as I had prayed he would, and we exchanged choicest insults of the purest Brussels vintage, none of which lend themselves to translation. During this performance I deliberately turned my back on the corporal, who finally remembered the word he wanted in French. He happily tapped me on the shoulder and, pointing again to the suitcase, managed to enunciate, "Uffrrear."

Suddenly, as if seeing the light, I exclaimed, "Oh! You mean open the valise? But, of course! How silly of me not to have guessed that right away! Of course I'll open it! Let me get my key!" He may not have followed my rapid patter, but I accompanied the words with significant gestures. I opened my purse and eagerly fumbled inside.

Still rummaging and smiling, I knelt down and emptied its considerable contents on the sidewalk, putting each piece back item by item with exaggerated care, as if the key were surely there.

The people behind me were now complaining loudly about the delay, and the line-up of other trams behind ours was steadily growing. Finally an officer came over to ask our corporal about the hold-up. The corporal, after saluting and clicking his heels, reported that I could not seem to find the key to my valise. The officer turned to me and in atrocious French asked, "Vat hef you in falisse?"

I smiled brightly. "What do I have inside? Just some potatoes, a little butter, a few goodies for my mother. She is ill in bed and I had to do the shopping for her."

The officer evidently wished to impress the corporal with his command of French, for he said to him, "The kid is only carrying some foodstuffs. Let her go. We've wasted too much time as it is. There are four tramcars backed up behind this one. We have to keep moving." With a flick of his hand he dismissed me.

I lost no time in grabbing my case and boarding the car again. The soldier watched me closely. I shall never forget the suspicion and disbelief in his eyes. Without a superior officer present, I knew he would never have let me pass so easily, but he had to obey orders. Thank heavens for army discipline. Only when the car began to move again did I slightly relax. By the grace of God and a little wit, I had escaped disaster, but only just.

This time I chose to remain standing on the open platform with a number of other passengers, including the burly heckler, who continued to scowl at me. The car's route was familiar to me. In a few minutes the tram would slow down before taking a sharp curve into the next thoroughfare. One of my impulses seized me. I pulled out my key while the passengers idly watched, swiftly unlocked the valise on my bent knees, and yanked it open wide for all to see its contents. At the same time I cried, "So you want to know what was inside? Have a good look!" Before they had time to recover from their shock, I slammed the case shut and leapt off the car as it slowed for the turn. I fled along a side street and walked the rest of the way to the station on foot, despite the heat. I felt better then than I had felt for a long time.

I entered the waiting-room with some five minutes to spare. The soldier was sitting on the right bench, with the twin valise at his feet. He had placed his folded greatcoat on the bench beside him, to discreetly reserve the seat for me. When I sat down, setting down my valise next to his, he casually tossed the coat over his lap, obscuring both cases from view. Then he looked at his watch, rose, seized my case, and strode off towards the waiting 4:55 train. The station clock read 4:54. I waited fifteen minutes longer, checked the remaining valise, and took a taxi back to Franz's apartment in good time.

I could not resist recounting my adventure to him. Predictably he raved and ranted and vowed he would never trust me again with such an errand. Thus ended my courier career.

12

Rotten Apples

The truism that war brings out the best in some people and the worst in others cannot be repeated too often. Jews are no exception to this rule. I personally encountered one Jewish informer who was a particularly offensive individual, known simply as Jacques.

Jacques was a brutish-looking, six-foot, three-hundred-pound hulk of a man who had worked as both a porter and a bouncer in a sleazy night-club near the Gare du Nord before the war. That area of town was equivalent to a red-light district in those days. Jacques spoke broken French, bad Flemish, and some German mixed with Yiddish. Some years before the war he had emigrated from Poland. I knew no more of his background than that. Whatever the rest of his personal history was, I considered him a poor specimen of humanity.

In 1943 he and his family were picked up by the Gestapo. To save his own skin, he volunteered to turn informer on his co-religionists, promising, as he phrased it, "to pick up every Jew in town". The Gestapo freed him on that condition, and he co-operated with them openly and fiercely, while his wife and children were shipped away to a death camp.

He possessed the uncanny ability to spot a Jew, male or female, at a glance, and from a considerable distance. And he rarely made a mistake. He began to roam the streets of Brussels, followed by a slowly cruising Gestapo car; when he spotted a Jew, he would grab and hold his quarry until the Gestapo hauled the individual away. His new masters soon decided that this procedure was too slow, and they ordered him to sit in the car with them and identify his prey less conspicuously as they patrolled the city streets. By this means they caught a fairly large number of Jewish people over the course of several months.

I first learned of Jacques's existence from Franz, who had seen him several times at Gestapo headquarters, waiting to collect his informer's salary. On one such occasion, Franz and I happened to be standing in the hall downstairs, so Franz pointed him out for me. I tried to memorize the man's face for the future. I found it vulgar and expressionless, the very image of a thug. He wore a pork-pie hat, a beige raincoat, and dark brown pants, in an obvious attempt to identify with the plainclothes Gestapo. No one ever saw him wear anything else. Gradually I heard more about Jacques and his treachery, and I repeatedly urged Franz to have him executed. He waved away my request many times with the excuse that he had more important jobs to do for London and the Resistance. I had no idea what these important jobs were. When I asked him, he replied he was sworn to secrecy.

Around ten o'clock one morning, I was waiting in the downstairs hall for the elevator to take me to the eighth floor, when Jacques approached me, his eyes fixed on my face with his vacant stare. He stopped in front of me and proclaimed, in his Yiddish-accented French, "You are Jewish! Follow me!"

I pretended not to know him and asked indignantly, "And who are you?"

He ignored my question and repeated mechanically, "You are Jewish. Come with me."

I recovered my composure sufficiently to laugh loudly in his face. "Are you out of your mind? I am German, an Aryan." As I spoke, I saw Schwenke coming towards the elevator. I raised my voice and spoke in German so that he would hear me. "How dare you insult me, you filthy Jew! And what right have *you* to be here, anyway?!"

As Schwenke was in earshot, I addressed him before he could say anything. "Herr Schwenke, this verdammter dirty Jew has insulted me! I demand that he be arrested immediately!"

As if he had heard nothing, Jacques turned to the officer and repeated dully, "She is Jewish. She has to follow me."

Schwenke assumed this was a joke and laughed. "Look here,

Jacques," he said. "Do you know who this Fräulein is? She is German, Aryan, and betrothed to one of our officers. Understand?"

Jacques remained completely unperturbed and continued to stare at me, repeating confidently, "She is Jewish."

To my complete surprise, Schwenke lost his temper. "You don't know what you are talking about, du Schweinehund! I know this Fräulein personally from Stuttgart. Now go away!" Although Jacques shuffled off, I knew he was not convinced.

For the life of me, I did not know how he could have guessed I was Jewish. I was ash blonde, with no distinctively Jewish features or traits that I knew of, and I had always passed easily for an Aryan, especially since I spoke German as fluently as a native.

The captain turned to me. "Sorry about this, Fräulein Olga. You see, we keep the Jew Jacques as a kind of dog, a pointer, to sniff out Jews. He is usually very good at it, but sometimes he makes mistakes." Schwenke smiled with a companionable shrug. I smiled gratefully in return, though the incident had greatly unnerved me.

When I was alone with Franz later, I told him about the encounter. He listened thoughtfully and delivered an unexpected verdict. "Then we shall have to get rid of that individual, and the sooner the better." I suspected that his sudden change of heart could not be entirely attributed to a concern for my personal security. He knew that his own safety depended on mine, and my second encounter with Jacques could be more than merely embarrassing to us both. We agreed to devise a plan of action that, I insisted, should include Jean and his Resistance friends.

For some reason I felt safer whenever Jean assisted in our exploits. Despite our role as a team at the Gestapo, I was finding that I did not trust Franz as much as I once had. If I had been asked at the time to explain my feelings I would have found it hard to be specific. During our many months together, I had gradually noticed certain attitudes of his that I had not noticed in our earlier friendship. He seemed to be developing a more cynical outlook on life, and a disturbing callousness.

His indifference about my financial straits, for example, was typical. And I did not understand his excessive secretiveness about himself. I wondered whether the war was to blame for these changes, or whether I had just never known the real Franz. As a result, my own feelings towards him were variable. Some days I felt confident and relatively secure with him; on others I was instinctively on my guard, especially when we were alone together on a mission. To ease my vague discomfort, I increasingly tried to ensure that someone else, such as Jean, accompanied us.

Our first task in eliminating Jacques was to find out where he lived. I was chosen to follow him. For this assignment I would need a great deal of time and so I once again had to report sick to my employer. By this time I had been absent for so long that Mme de Herrandt wanted to replace me. Her sympathetic husband, however, was a gentleman possessed of a longer memory. He insisted that I be kept on. I appreciated his intervention deeply for I desperately needed the salary.

To shadow Jacques, I had to change my appearance beyond recognition. Jean arranged an appointment for me with a ladies' hairdresser on the rue des Bouchers, in the theatre district. He took me there when the place had closed for lunch, an old European tradition rapidly disappearing. The hairdresser, a friend of his, admitted us, carefully locking the door behind him. He led us through the salon to a back room concealed behind a sliding panel that merged perfectly with the salon wall. The room hidden behind was in fact a make-up shop replete with an incredible assortment of creams, paints, wigs, props, and apparel of every kind—in short, everything required for either a stage appearance or a disguise. Jean's friend was an artist in his own right. In very little time he had transformed me into a brunette with a face and dark glasses that bore no resemblance to the face I had always known in mirrors. He even fitted me out with a jacket and skirt to match, to complete the effect.

I started my job that same evening, at six o'clock sharp, just before Jacques was expected to leave the Gestapo building. From a discreet distance, I watched him emerge at ten past the hour and walk straight to the tramcar stop. I boarded the same car, keeping out of his sight, and when he alighted at the porte de Namur ten minutes later, so did I. I pretended to fumble in my bag while he waited for a connecting tram. His car arrived and he boarded it. At the last moment I hopped on and found that there was only one seat available. To my consternation I found myself directly facing my quarry. He did not take any notice of me, however, nor of anyone else. In an eerie way his eyes seemed to be turned inwards, and I fancied that he was sufficiently gorged with blood to rest after the day's efforts. The car stopped twenty minutes later at the Midi station, which was its terminal point, and all passengers disembarked.

This would be the difficult part. In the gathering dusk I had to follow him on foot, at an inconspicuous distance, through the almost deserted streets. He finally paused before a tenement house and automatically turned to see if anyone had been following him. I walked briskly by on the other side of the street, reassured that he would probably have expected to see a man following him, if anyone. I slowed down and blew my nose, turning just in time to see him opening the door with a key and disappearing inside. I knew a person who suspects that someone is following him will deliberately enter one house and then leave shortly after for his real destination, so I waited there for a full half-hour. When he still had not come out, I called Jean from a nearby café and asked him to meet me there.

Then I sat down and ordered a café-filtre and a bun, a small luxury that I vaguely hoped to recoup from Franz. Twenty minutes later Jean joined me, accompanied by a friend. I indicated the house, and Jean instructed his colleague to keep it under observation every evening between six and ten until further notice.

After three days, we received confirmation that Jacques returned home every evening around seven and did not go out again. At our next meeting, Franz was chosen to act as executioner the following day, which was a Thursday. On that evening, Franz picked me up in his car and, with Jean and Jean's assistant, we set out. The assistant and I were to serve as witnesses, as underground tradition demanded when traitors were to be given their due.

We parked around the corner from his street, from which point we could see him coming. It was already dark when his bulky outline appeared around the corner. By the time he reached his building, our car was stealthily following him, with Jean now at the wheel. Franz had his gun and silencer ready. When Jacques turned his back to the street to insert his key in the lock, the car passed him and braked. Franz leaped out right behind him and fired all six bullets into the man's back, all within a few seconds. Much elated, we congratulated Franz as he rejoined us, leaving the man silent and motionless on the curb. I personally felt greatly relieved that this informer was out of the way.

But we later learned that he was not dead when we left him, nor did he die of his bullet wounds. He was carried to a hospital and operated on immediately. By some twist of fate, every bullet had missed the vital organs, and all were successfully extracted. After some six weeks in hospital, Jacques was back on the street again, still wearing the same old beige raincoat, but with several bullet holes in it, a decoration of which he was very proud.

It was not possible for us to try once again to execute him. While in hospital, he was guarded twenty-four hours a day, and only the doctor and nurse on duty were allowed near him. When he recovered, he promptly moved to a new address and never again travelled by public transportation. The Gestapo chauffeured him to and from home or paid his taxi fare. In such circumstances, to track, corner, and dispatch him would have involved too many additional risks for us, and the Resistance had other concerns.

At long last most of the remaining Jews in town kept off the streets of Brussels, particularly in broad daylight. Jacques found fewer and fewer victims and became less and less useful to the Gestapo, until he was seldom seen. A little before D-Day, he disappeared altogether, either eliminated by the Gestapo itself or finally shipped off to die in a concentration camp. In either case, no one ever heard of him again.

I also encountered another traitor, in a more familiar context. He happened to be a Gentile and a member of the same Resistance group to which Jean belonged. Actually Franz and Jean caught him; I was only an accessory.

Franz told me one day that he had met a suspicious character at one of the small cafés near the porte Louise, which he often patronized for the purpose of picking up odd pieces of information. The man was a regular customer who was adept at encouraging patrons to talk freely to him. Franz was sure he had seen the fellow's face before, but he could not remember where. He was concerned enough about the man to ask me to go to the café myself, get friendly with him, and find out who he was and what he wanted. I agreed, on condition that I go with Jean, and play it by ear from there.

It was arranged that Franz, in his Gestapo uniform, would sit alone at one of the tables, and Jean and I would walk in a few minutes later and choose an empty table next to his. If our man was there, Franz would point him out to us by a prearranged signal. If not, we were to inconspicuously watch the entrance. As soon as the man appeared, Franz would drop his glass of beer on the floor. There was no guarantee, of course, that he would turn up that evening, so we were prepared to repeat the exercise the following evening.

When we took our seats in the café that evening, Franz signalled that our man had not yet arrived. Jean ordered a café-filtre for me and a beer for himself, and we watched the door. Patrons passed steadily in and out, but we received no signal from the neighbouring table. Around eight-thirty, however, a glass of beer crashed on the floor beside us as a man walked in. The newcomer was a man in his thirties, short and squat, and wearing a workman's cap and clothes. As soon as Jean saw him he whipped his head away, exclaiming under his breath, "Oh my God! It's Jeff! He mustn't see me! Olga, let's get out of here, quick!" Franz followed us soon after, very curious to know what was the matter. Jean refused to speak until we were back in the safety of his apartment, where he told us a grim story.

About a year earlier, a section of his group, some fifteen men including Jeff and Jean, had agreed to meet in a house near place Fontainas. Everyone but Jeff had been there on time. They did not wait for him, but proceeded with their business. Hardly fifteen minutes later, they heard unusual noises outside, and then the front door was broken down. A handful of Jean's men had not reached the back exit by the time the first of the Gestapo men burst into the house. All but four Resistance members managed to escape through the back door. In the exchange of fire that followed, the four men were killed.

The maquisards were never quite certain who had betrayed them, though the conspicuously absent Jeff was strongly suspected. Since he had disappeared completely, however, he was presumed dead—until this evening when Jean saw him at the café. Now he was sure that the man was a traitor. He also remembered having once shown Franz a snapshot of Jeff, together with several photographs of other men who had disappeared, and this must have explained why Franz thought he had seen his face before.

We returned to the café the following evening. This time Jean was a redhead, complete with moustache and beard, compliments of his artistic hairdresser friend. Franz arrived a few minutes later and again sat at a table near ours. Jeff was already there, standing at the bar counter, a glass of beer in his hand.

At an appropriate moment, Jean raised his glass, complaining loudly that he did not like the café's beer and wanted another drink. He asked if anyone wanted a free beer, and then, vaguely offering the glass in Jeff's direction, asked him if he wanted the extra beer at no charge. Jeff accepted very readily.

When he came to fetch his drink I invited him with my most engaging smile to sit with us. Flattered, he accepted. We shook hands and Jean made the introductions. Jeff introduced himself as Tintin, which struck me as funny, since I had once had a teddy bear by the same name. I said so, and we all laughed, which helped to break the ice.

While we sipped our drinks, Jean remarked that Tintin looked very much like a fellow he knew whose name was Jeff. I watched the latter carefully for his reaction to this broadside and thought I noticed a fleeting shadow of fear in his eyes. He quickly regained his composure, however, and answered simply that, no, he was not Jeff, he was Tintin. He smiled to end the discussion. I felt instinctively that he was lying.

We changed subjects and talked of other things. Jean, who knew that Jeff was an avid chess-player, carefully steered the conversation towards games, mentioning in passing that he himself was very partial to chess, but rarely had the chance to play it these days. When he turned to Tintin, the latter took the bait and answered that sure, he played chess, it was his favourite game. Jean knew the café had sets available for the use of its patrons and so asked if he cared to play a game. Tintin looked delighted.

Jean summoned the owner and ordered a chess set with another round of drinks. When the board arrived, we were reminded that the bar closed in about an hour, in accordance with the eleven o'clock curfew. Looking up from the chessmen he was setting up, Tintin announced defiantly, "I'll go when I bloody well like, never mind no curfews!" I wondered at the outburst and asked, innocently enough, if he carried a permit with him. He answered no, he did not, and he did not believe in curfews: "To hell with them!"

I guessed that he was trying to find out our reactions to his apparently rebellious attitude. I decided to throw him off. Loudly enough that Franz could overhear me, I said that I had no permit and no intention of getting arrested, and that if my companions wanted to stay, they were welcome; but I would be leaving at a quarter to eleven. Franz approached our table and casually introduced himself. He had overheard our conversation, he said, and was a chess-player himself. He would love to watch the game, if the players did not mind, and added that, if they wished, they could stay past curfew time. He would be very pleased to drive us all home himself in his car.

I invited him to sit with us, and the game began. Promptly at eleven the owner locked the door for the night and left us in our German officer's care. Franz and I watched the players, the two of us exchanging polite platitudes, which I found highly amusing under the circumstances. A little before midnight Jean reluctantly conceded the game to Tintin, rose from his seat, and stretched. Franz asked us where we lived, and after some discussion, it was decided that he would drop Jean off first. The drive to Jean's apartment was uneventful. When Franz parked in front of the building, I suggested we all go in for a cup of coffee or a last drink before parting. Our unsuspecting guest happily welcomed the suggestion.

We had hardly seated ourselves in the parlour when Jean dropped all pretence with Tintin. "Look here, I am positive that your name is Jeff. Isn't that right?" Our suspect looked a little uneasy, but insisted stoutly that his name was Tintin, as he had already told us. Jean retorted that this was really strange, considering that when he had met him before, with the other men about a year ago, his name had been Jeff. He reminded him of the meeting in the place Fontainas, adding that Tintin not only looked like Jeff but talked like him, with the same Flemish accent.

Tintin held his ground. He pretended not to know what Jean was talking about and maintained Jean had made a mistake. At this point, Jean removed his wig, moustache, and beard, and asked, "Do you recognize me now, Jeff?"

Jeff still did not give in. He slowly turned his head, looking at each of us in turn. We silently stared back at him. His voice sounded a little shakier now. "What is this, a trap of some kind?"

"Well, yes, if you want to call it that," said Jean. "You still deny that your name is Jeff?"

Jeff did: his name was, and remained, Tintin. He knew very well by this time that his only chance lay in denying his real identity.

Jean told him he would have to appear before the Resistance command, where he would be thoroughly interrogated and checked out. If he was Tintin, he had nothing to fear; but if he was Jeff, then "ton compte est bon". The man now looked really scared, but remained silent. Franz, standing on guard in his Gestapo uniform with his hand on his holster, was an intimidating figure. Jean ordered Tintin to follow us quietly and without fuss. Our informer could only meekly obey, Jean preceding him and Franz behind.

Jean and Franz drove Jeff to a neighbouring house, where he was given into the care of an underground member, who promised to guard him before handing him over to the Namur chief the following day.

In the meantime, I remained in the apartment, waiting for my partners to return. I was hungry and weary in body and spirit, especially as my one meal a day at the Herrandts' was hardly adequate to keep me going until late at night. I had used up my meagre rations for the month more than a week ago and could not afford to buy extra food on the black market. Pride prevented me from requesting any money from Franz, since he had refused to help me on the two previous occasions when I had asked for money so that I could eat. Although he complained of being short of cash himself, I knew the

Gestapo paid him well. He enjoyed fringe benefits that included free lodgings, the use of a car, and more. Most of the people I knew at the time outside the Resistance and the Nazi regime, people like my sister and brother-in-law, barely survived and lived from hand to mouth.

I somehow managed to cope with the daily demands of this precarious existence, but I could never get used to the pangs of hunger. My desire for food became an obsession, which I have never completely overcome. Even now, some forty years later, I must still check a tendency to buy more than I need at the supermarket and to prepare quantities of food considerably in excess of my family's eating capacity. And despite this, my weight has never exceeded one hundred pounds.

While I awaited Jean's and Franz's return that night, I went to prowl hungrily through Jean's kitchen, which I had never seen before. I was surprised to find that the place had been converted into some sort of storage room. It was cluttered with tools, equipment, and all kinds of odd pieces. Dirty cups were piled in the sink; an empty enamelled coffee-pot stood on the cold stove, beside a mouldy crust of bread. On the one and only shelf in the cupboard not loaded with non-edible paraphernalia, I found an old hand-operated coffee-grinder, a nearly empty bag of coffee beans, an unopened bottle of beer, and a cup containing five or six lumps of sugar, one of which I guiltily stole. Jean obviously did not eat at home very often. I realized that he was probably not much better off than I was.

Jean and Franz walked in half an hour later, having left Jeff in secure hands. Jean excused himself for not being able to offer us anything but beer, which we politely refused. Soon after, Franz drove me home, and I went to bed around two in the morning, still hungry.

Jeff's fate was predictable. Several survivors of the raid at place Fontainas identified Tintin as Jeff beyond any doubt. After futile denials, he finally confessed; he was tried by his peers, found guilty of treason, and shot. One cannot be sentimental about such decisions in wartime, when the lives of your friends and often your own life are at stake.

These encounters with traitors inevitably broadened my perceptions. But, interesting though my minor role in these incidents was, it could not compare with the part I was called upon to play soon afterwards.

13

A Final Solution

Hauptsturmführer Schwenke of the Gestapo was not only ambitious but envious. He plotted and schemed in hopes of earning his promotion to lieutenant colonel, which would place him on an equal footing with Mueller, his superior officer, whose post he coveted. He was notorious at avenue Louise for his zeal and ruthlessness, and he exacted the maximum performance from his underlings. He was forever snooping around, eager to find fault with everyone, suspecting others of the same plots and dreams of rich rewards as his own. This was finally to be his undoing.

I was first made aware of Schwenke's scheming mind the day after Mueller had left for Germany on a two-week furlough. Schwenke asked me to translate into French a notice to be published in the local newspaper, *Le Soir*, then under German control. The notice proclaimed that a reward of forty Belgian francs would be paid to any citizen whose information resulted in the arrest of a Jew; letters were to be addressed to the Brussels Gestapo, eighth floor, avenue Louise. Those entitled to the reward would collect it in person.

When I handed Schwenke the translation, inwardly seething with rage, he informed me it would now be my job to manage the whole business. I understood that to mean not only going to *Le Soir* to have the ad published but also translating all incoming mail from the would-be informers and passing the information on for action. I would also have to pay the traitors their pieces of silver. All this was to be in addition to my usual chores for Franz.

I could not bring myself to undertake the disgusting task, and I had a valid excuse ready. "Herr Schwenke, I believe this is a full-time job. As you know, I can only spare two half-days a week at the office. So it looks as if Leutnant Boehler will have to take charge of this."

The man did not look pleased at all and replied, scowling, "Fräulein Olga, I am curious to know what is really so important in your life that keeps you busy all week and leaves so little time for your duty to the Vaterland."

A shrewd question, but I had the answer ready: "As I explained to Oberst Mueller, I am under doctor's orders not to overexert myself, owing to a heart condition. That is why I cannot work full-time."

He scanned me thoroughly and inquired, with a touch of sarcasm, whether I was in the hands of a good doctor. He suggested that I have myself thoroughly examined by one of the Gestapo's own doctors. "They are excellent, you know," he said, "and you won't have to pay anything."

Feeling trapped, I bluffed my way out by taking the offensive. "Oberst Mueller is well aware of my health problem and agreed to my offer of working part-time only, as an unpaid volunteer. And I am not supposed to receive orders for full-time jobs. That is why, if you wish to have the job done properly, you will have to hand it over to Leutnant Boehler, or to someone else."

He grumbled that for such a small person, I certainly had a big mouth. He used a vulgar expression, however, more akin to "snout" than to "mouth". I pretended to take exception to the remark, murmured something like, "If you feel that way about me . . . ," and left his office, slightly slamming the door behind me.

Although my bluff apparently worked that time, I felt uneasy about Schwenke. So, in fact, did Franz; during those two weeks of the assistant's rule, he came into the office only sporadically, pretending to be on the trail of some spies. He tried to avoid the captain as much as possible, though he was nevertheless saddled with the job that had originally been assigned to me. Claiming that such tasks were beneath his dignity, he in turn delegated an underling in another office to carry it out, a sergeant who dutifully placed the ad and received the resulting mail. When the letters began to pour in, they were referred by the sergeant to our office. Eventually we had to place some of the mail on Mueller's desk, where it accumulated until a higher decision was made.

Thanks to all these delays, and to the fact that few Jews stayed long in one place, quite a number of those reported had time to change their hide-outs before the Gestapo reached them. But too many failed to get away. And after a while, the informers began calling to collect their forty francs. As we were the only French-speaking personnel in that Gestapo section, Franz and I were assigned the unpleasant task of paying them off. We decided that each informer would require an appointment to collect his money, one that had to coincide with Franz's presence, or mine, at the office. This enabled us to copy the informers' names and addresses onto a list, which I passed on to Jean. He relayed the names to Resistance headquarters, and they were filed for future reference and retribution, sometimes even after the war.

I remember one repulsive individual in particular whose account had to be settled long before the Liberation. He reported to our office on six different occasions, each time to collect his forty pieces of silver. For this Judas we requested special treatment from the maquis, who responded with speed and efficiency. A few days after he had collected his sixth, and last, cheque, two men quietly called at his home and slit his throat from ear to ear, as a warning to others.

During Mueller's absence in Germany, new developments forced Franz and me to make a crucial decision concerning Schwenke. Some time earlier Schwenke had revealed to an officer in a different section that he did not like or trust Leutnant Boehler. He considered him something of a playboy, shirking his duties and having a good time at the expense of the Gestapo. The lieutenant's missions were suspiciously vague, he said, and he meant to have him closely watched. He had no intention, he confided, of mentioning anything to Mueller until he could collect some concrete evidence against Franz. On another occasion he told the same officer that he would like to see Franz transferred to some other unit or service, as he did not produce enough solid work in his department.

All this was repeated to Franz over dinner and drinks by Schwenke's confidant, with whom Franz happened to be on friendly terms. For the officer, these confidences were nothing more than the usual insignificant barracks gossip. To Franz, however, they threatened imminent danger.

I had also sensed a certain change in the captain's attitude towards me. I attributed this to his own frustration, since I had consistently rejected his personal advances. Whatever the reason, I sensed that my own position was similarly threatened.

I learned of this new problem when I met Franz unexpectedly one day at the maquis camp near Namur. He was delivering arms and ammunition and looked very worried, which was rare for him. He said he was afraid he had been followed, though he had been very careful to shake off any possible tail. He thought he might have to stay away from Namur for a while.

Franz and I agreed that although Schwenke might suspect us only of playing truant, his persistence would sooner or later uncover far more damaging evidence of our other activities. Such a discovery would mean promotion for him, and arrest, torture, and an ugly death for us. On the other hand, if he succeeded in arranging Franz's transfer to another unit, or back to the Todt, and consequently my dismissal, our undercover work within the Gestapo would be ended. Our early warnings to those on the Gestapo lists and our assistance in their escape were far too important to abandon without a fight.

Together we resolved to put a stop to Schwenke's interference; we called a meeting with Jean and René, an underground chief. The vote was unanimous. The man was to be liquidated—and the sooner the better.

Franz had already made some preliminary inquiries about Schwenke's habits. He knew, for instance, that he spent almost every night with his mistress, a married woman whose husband, a collaborator, was absent from home for weeks at a time, dealing in supplies for the German army. She lived in a luxurious mansion on the edge of the forêt de Soignes, in a neighbourhood of wealthy homes. Her lover had an apartment on the chic avenue des Nations not far away, and he generally walked home in the morning through a short cut in the forest. Further surveillance was required to reinforce this information. The Resistance readily offered to provide the necessary female personnel. We were to await their report in a few days' time before choosing our next course of action.

On his return from Germany, Mueller installed a secretary in our office, at the instigation of his assistant, Schwenke. This was done on the pretext that Franz now needed a full-time employee to supplement my part-time contribution, which was considered insufficient for the volume of work. Schwenke obviously intended this third party to keep him informed about how we spent our time at the office. The new arrangement weakened our position considerably, but it also put us on our guard and forced us to tighten our security precautions.

The new secretary was a woman in her forties, fat, ugly, and, to me, repulsive. I disliked her cold snake-eyes and her thin pursed mouth. She pretended to know French, but we soon discovered that her knowledge of the language was somewhat less than elementary. Whatever her knowledge of written French, she could not follow the spoken word at all, claiming that people were talking too fast—a common excuse of those not fluent in a foreign language.

Within a few days we heard from the Resistance. Girls had been sent to the forêt de Soignes, ostensibly to pick berries in the woods, while they spied on the home of Schwenke's mistress and on Schwenke himself. They had accomplished their task well, for they were able to confirm that our friend left his mistress's house every morning just before eight and took a short cut home along a trail in the forest. The trail seemed completely deserted at all times, except on weekends. All we needed now was to choose the day and time, the weapon, and the executioner. We all agreed that no gun was to be used, as this could result in the shooting of hostages. The executioner would have to carry a knife, stab the officer to death, and remove his wallet and wrist-watch. His papers and revolver were not to be touched, as the attack had to look like a mugging and murder by a common criminal.

I was still in bed when the doorbell rang the morning after these plans had been settled. My landlady, who had not yet left for work, opened the door and called out, "Madame Andrée! A gentleman to see you!" I slipped on my robe and went downstairs, curious. Franz was there, dressed in civilian clothes. Mme de Bruyn had never seen him before, so I introduced him as a friend of my brother-in-law.

I asked him to wait until I was dressed, and then we walked to his car. His opening words stunned me: "Olga, you have been chosen to kill Schwenke."

All I could find to say was, "Why me?"

"First of all let me tell you that the choice was unanimous. The boys agreed with me that the executioner must be someone well known to Schwenke. He would not allow any stranger near him, especially since he doesn't speak French. And he must be caught by surprise. So it will have to be you. An ambush was suggested but rejected because it could end in a shooting match, and that's the last thing we want, as you well know."

As I remained silent, he added, "You understand that you must not treat this as a personal vendetta; it must be absolutely impersonal, and dictated purely by the security of our cover." I nodded, and asked when.

"Tomorrow morning. It's not safe to wait any longer. I'm afraid you'll have to take a few more days off from your employers. It can't be helped."

"What about a weapon? And a briefing?"

"Jean gave me a sharp dagger for you. I have it at home. I'll pick you up after work this afternoon and drive you to the forest for a briefing and a rehearsal on the spot. You'll also need a change of clothes for tomorrow. We may have to burn what you'll be wearing if there are any blood stains."

"All right. But I can't afford to buy new clothes myself. You know very well that I'm broke."

"OK. I'll buy you new clothes." The offer impressed me and I looked at him sharply. Certainly the captain's death would benefit him as much as, if not more than, it would me.

He had prepared another surprise. He told me that I was to pack a small valise with whatever I needed for one night, as I would have to spend the night in his apartment. I found the arrangement puzzling. At first I thought he intended to make me go to bed with him. Knowing Franz, however, I should have realized he had something else on his mind. I asked him if he was afraid I might change my mind during the night. He replied briefly that his place was much nearer to the forêt de Soignes than mine. This would save a lot of driving back and forth so early in the morning, when we would be pressed for time. It made sense.

At work I faked flu symptoms and left early. Mme de Herrandt was most concerned, and she easily agreed with my suggestion that I might have to stay in bed for a few days.

Franz came to fetch me in the afternoon. After buying my new clothes, we drove to a lonely spot in the woods and parked the car. From there we walked until we found the trail that Schwenke was supposed to follow each morning. After some further exploration, we chose a convenient site for the execution. We went through all the possible motions at the very tree stump where I was to sit the next morning, nursing an imaginary sprained ankle.

Night had fallen by the time we returned to Franz's apartment, having stopped somewhere for a quick snack. Though I turned in early, I could not sleep. I paced my room up and down until late into the night, tormented by doubts about the gruesome task ahead of me. To kill "impersonally"—and with a knife, at that—is much easier said than done. I tried to overcome my scruples and natural revulsion by reminding myself of Schwenke's odious crimes and sadistic tortures. I thought of my helpless parents, deported to a death camp, and of the multitude of other victims, men, women, and children, whose blood seemed to cry to me for vengeance. Finally, having justified my mission to myself, I was able to go to sleep.

Dawn arrived all too soon that dreaded morning. When I was ready to go, Franz handed the dagger over to me, and I placed it in my handbag. He offered some final advice: "Just in case the attempt is botched, and you find yourself trapped and unable to escape, yell 'Away' at the top of your voice, so that I'll hear you and can get away. There's no point in both of us being sacrificed." These words made me realize, with chilling clarity, how risky and foolhardy a scheme we had devised. It also reinforced my impression that Franz cared very little for other people and, in particular, for me. He did not even give me an encouraging hug or a word of comfort. All my doubts of the long night before returned, but I knew there was no turning back.

Just before seven we parked the car at the same secluded spot as the day before; this time I set off alone on foot while Franz remained in the car, waiting for me. I soon reached the trail and the stump on which I had been sitting little more than twelve hours earlier. With a few handfuls of dirt, I rubbed over my stockings and different parts of my clothes to simulate the marks of a fall. Then I sat down, removed one shoe, and waited to discover my fate and that of my victim.

The suspense was nearly intolerable. I felt suddenly sick to my stomach and weak in the knees, and I remember thinking, "What a time to get sick; now I won't have to fake any pain." I sat there for what seemed like hours, listening to the rustle of the forest around me and wishing simultaneously that Schwenke would come soon and that he would not come at all.

I gave a start when I heard whistling in the distance. As the whistler came into view, still far away from my clearing, I recognized Schwenke's strutting gait. By now I had recovered my calm and was ready for action. He could not have been more than a few yards away when he recognized me sitting there, nursing my ankle.

"Why, Fräulein Olga!" he exclaimed. "What in heaven's name are *you* doing here, at this time of day?"

I retorted, unabashed, "And what are *you* doing here so early, Herr Schwenke?"

"Well, I was staying with some friends in the neighbourhood and decided to take a morning stroll through the woods."

"What a coincidence! Franz had to go to Genval, so I asked him to drop me near the forest on his way. I love the forest at this time of year, but today I was foolish to come."

"Why? What's happened?"

"I think I've sprained my ankle. I was watching some birds—cardinals, I think—when I stumbled and fell. It was silly of me." While talking I kept rubbing my ankle and grimacing as if in pain. He came closer, looking at my foot.

"Are you sure you can't walk?"

"I don't know."

"Have you tried?" I stood experimentally but as soon as I put weight on my "bad" ankle I let out a cry of pain. He looked at my ankle again and suggested tentatively, "Massaging would probably help."

"I am not much good at that, I'm afraid. Perhaps you could do it for me, please?" I smiled warmly and he knelt and started massaging my ankle. I was appropriately grateful and said, "Oh, that's *much* better, thank you. I don't know what I would have done, here all alone, if I had not met you." While he massaged he remarked matter-of-factly that the forest was no place for a girl to walk all alone, and that this should be a lesson to me. He asked me again to try to walk. I pretended to feel somewhat better, but thought a little more massaging might do the trick.

I don't know what he could have been thinking, but he obligingly knelt again, to resume his massaging. While he bent his head, I thought, "Now or never." I grabbed the dagger from my open bag and, swinging my arm upward, thrust the knife deep into his abdomen with full force. He let out a loud groan of pain, and as he tried to draw himself up, I yanked the knife out and stabbed him repeatedly, savagely, blindly, while saying to myself, "That's for all the Jews you've killed, and for all the other Gestapo atrocities!"

His eyes were wide open and fixed on me in surprise. He made a desperate effort to scream, but all I heard was a gurgle from deep down in his throat. His blood oozed and spurted all over me. He collapsed on his stomach and lay quite still. As if in a trance, I wiped the knife on his sleeve, searched his pockets until I found his wallet, undid his wrist-watch, and threw the lot into my bag. I replaced my shoe, seized the bag, and started running madly, dodging the trail and zigzagging amongst the trees in terror of being seen. I saw and felt blood everywhere—on my clothes, on my hands, on my face. In panic I suddenly could not remember where Franz's car was located: "Oh my God! I'm lost! What shall I do now?" I ran on, panting and desperate, until miraculously I recognized the path that led to the waiting car.

When Franz saw me, all he said was, "You've been a hell of a long time! It must have been quite a butchery! You're covered in blood! Is he dead?"

I resented his remarks and snarled, "How should I know? I didn't have time to check his heart!" I scrambled into the back of the car, wiped off the worst of the blood, and changed my clothes while Franz drove, heading for his apartment. I went straight to the bathroom there and showered furiously, frantic to wash away the last vestiges of blood. Meanwhile, my soiled skirt, blouse, and stockings were burning in the fireplace, together with Schwenke's wrist-watch and the wallet. The money we kept.

Since we had no means of checking whether Schwenke was dead or still alive, my only alternative was to remain in hiding until we knew for sure. If he had survived the attack, Franz and I would both have to disappear into the maquis for good.

Later that day Jean drove me to a safe place in Schaerbeek, north of Brussels, where I stayed with an elderly couple whose son had belonged to the underground. A few months earlier he had been caught by the Boches and shot. These charitable people pampered me so much that the three peaceful days I spent there were worth three weeks' rest elsewhere. The good woman prepared scrumptious meals for me, the like of which I had almost forgotten: rich soups, thick juicy steaks, fresh vegetables, home-made pies. I had milk, real butter, home-made bread. She must have obtained extra ration stamps from the Resistance and received extra food from some farm. Although everything, all the way up to caviar and lobster, could be obtained through the black market, the prices had always been far beyond my own means. My fare since 1943 had consisted mostly of boiled potatoes and herring, when it was in season and plentiful, as my monthly allotment of food stamps sufficed for only two or three hearty meals. When you are deprived of these staples, you learn to savour every little crumb. While I rested, I dreamed of being free and able to live a normal life again. I felt exhausted, but once enmeshed in an underground network, one can retreat or escape only through death.

The body was discovered a full two days later, by an anonymous cyclist who phoned the Belgian police. When identification had been confirmed, the police advised the Gestapo, and the corpse was taken to their own morgue.

On the third day I received the all-clear signal, which meant that I could make a safe reappearance at the Gestapo office. Since I had often stayed away for several days on end, neither my absence nor my return caused any particular stir there. Our secretary, Frau Bertha, however, kept bemoaning the dear Hauptmann's foul murder. I pretended to sympathize with her, this woman who would not have batted an eye had a dozen Jewish children been slaughtered before her eyes. Franz and I dutifully attended the funeral.

Later that week I expressed my condolences to Mueller. He did not show much grief but actually criticized his late assistant for being so careless as to roam the woods by himself. He knew, of course, of Schwenke's liaison, and told Franz in private at one point that he did not believe the theory that Schwenke had been the victim of a mugging: he was sure that the cuckolded husband had had something to do with the murder. But the matter never went any further.

I had been lucky again, and Franz and I were now free to resume our activities unhindered and undetected. But I let both Franz and Jean know that they were not to rely on me for another mission like the last one. They tried to placate me with praises for my courage in carrying out the assignment. In fact I had to admit to myself that I did occasionally derive considerable satisfaction from my successful completion of a dangerous mission; but I never performed so grisly an assignment again. A few weeks later I was called upon to participate in yet another dangerous operation, but one of a very different nature.

14

Through Fort
and Forest

The small Belgian town of Dinant, near Namur, is perhaps most famous for its nine-hundred-year-old citadel, which is perched on a cliff overlooking the river Meuse far below, a sheer drop of three hundred feet. Seen from across the river, or from the air, it towers far above a beautiful old church and dwarfs the colourful eighteenth-century houses bordering the quay. The whole setting is considered one of the most picturesque sights in Belgium.

Through the centuries, and in the 1940s, the only means of reaching the fortress was by climbing the 408 steps hewn in the rock or by following a steep access road winding its way up through the densely wooded forest behind. Before the war, as now, the citadel housed a museum renowned for its collection of ancient armour, weapons, and historic artifacts. I remember visiting the place with our school in pre-war days. During the war, however, the Germans converted the lower level of the fortress into a temporary prison where captured Resistance members and other suspects were held before being transferred to other prisons or to concentration camps.

In September 1943, I was feeling very low, brooding about my parents and Albert, the weariness of this prolonged war, and my enforced diet of raw herring and cold potatoes. I needed some action to shake off my sense of gloom.

Then Franz called quite unexpectedly to tell me about a new mission. He had been assigned an important job by the Resistance chief and had prepared a coup in which I would have a part to play. About ten days earlier, a truck carrying some thirty Resistance workers was heading for France, where they were to join a maquis. On the way the vehicle was stopped by a detachment of Feldpolizei, the secret military police, before it had even left Belgium. The men realized then that they had been betrayed, because their captors asked no questions but simply arrested all of them and packed them off to the Dinant citadel, where they were jailed.

The Resistance had gathered information through its own channels that these particular prisoners were to be removed from the citadel on Saturday, September 18*, either for deportation to Germany or, worse, for interrogation by the Gestapo. With Franz's invaluable aid as a Gestapo officer, the Resistance had resolved to rescue the men before that date.

Franz would be able to appropriate the necessary transfer forms and official seals from Mueller's desk drawer, where they were kept, signed in advance and ready for use in Mueller's absence or in an emergency. Important orders required a second signature by another high-ranking officer. For this operation the second signature presented no problem. Franz had collected photographs of the important Gestapo signatures, which a Resistance engraver could forge perfectly.

A blank was duly filled out, stamped, dated, and signed, ready for our use. The rescue was set for Thursday, September 16, before midnight, as prisoners were usually transferred late at night.

On that Thursday, we arrived at Namur camp early in the evening. Franz wore his Gestapo uniform, and the three German-speaking colleagues who were to accompany us were outfitted as Wehrmacht soldiers. My uniform was too large for me at first, but a seamstress, summoned for the purpose, measured me and returned the garment within an hour, deftly altered to a perfect fit. With the addition of a Red Cross armband and nurse's cap, I became an instant Red Cross Blitzmädchen. According to our orders we were not to disclose our identity to the freed prisoners until our safe return to the camp, unless the men became openly rebellious or attempted to escape. If that point were reached, our refusal to reveal ourselves could jeopardize the whole operation.

We ate a hasty meal of fresh bacon and eggs, courtesy of local

* These dates may not be exact.

farmers sympathetic to the Resistance, and drank some substitute coffee. Following a final inspection, we left for the citadel, at 2100 hours sharp.

We passed through the Ardennes forest to the steep road leading to the citadel and slowly rumbled upwards. It was just after 2300 hours when we parked in front of the fortress doors. A lone soldier guarded the entrance. Franz and I jumped off the truck, exchanged salutes of "Heil Hitler" with the sentry, and showed the Gestapo pass. Franz entered while I remained at the entrance, chatting with the guard; two of our soldiers climbed down from the back of the truck and took up positions behind the vehicle, their Schmeissers at the ready. The third soldier stayed inside the otherwise empty truck. After we had exchanged a few pleasantries, the sentry let me pass. In the guardroom I found a non-commissioned Wehrmacht officer busily scrutinizing Franz's papers. These included an official order from Brussels Gestapo headquarters to the commanding officer of the citadel, instructing him to surrender all prisoners to Franz's custody for transportation to Germany. The document was properly stamped and signed by the chief and another officer. Reading the order through carefully, the NCO spoke respectfully to Franz but seemed hesitant. "Herr Leutnant, this is quite unexpected. The Kommandant told me the prisoners were to be transferred on the 18th, which is next Saturday."

"I have my orders," answered Franz, curtly, clipping his words. "You've seen them. They must be obeyed."

"Of course, Herr Leutnant, of course. I wish the Kommandant were here, though. If you will excuse me, I'll try to get hold of him at his home." So saying, he picked up the phone, called a number, and waited.

This was the critical moment for us. If the colonel were to be so suspicious as to come down to the fort, or to check with Gestapo headquarters, I was to return to the entrance and engage the sentry in conversation again. Franz was to follow me on some pretext as soon as he could, and I would in turn follow him into the truck. If necessary, we were prepared to run for the truck under cover of fire from our men and escape at full speed. Like all battle plans, this back-up strategy involved great danger, but we had no alternative.

At last the sergeant hung up the phone and sighed, "No answer."

Franz, now more confident, showed signs of impatience and spoke sharply to him. "Look here, I haven't got all night, and it's late enough. I must ask you to comply with Gestapo orders."

The sergeant clicked his heels, saluted, uttered a firm "Jawohl!"

and strode to the door to give the necessary commands to his men. As he passed me, he stopped abruptly, apparently noticing me for the first time, and asked in a surprised voice what I was doing there. Franz smoothly answered that according to regulations, a nurse had to be present on any trip involving such a large number of prisoners. The NCO apologized with Teutonic servility and continued on his way.

The inmates were brought out five at a time and prodded into the truck by our soldiers, who yelled, "Herein! Schnell machen!" The men understood the gestures, though not the language. To our surprise, we counted forty-five men, instead of the expected thirty. They had to be pressed into the truck like sardines, with barely enough room left for their two new guards and the "nurse". Time being short, no questions were asked about the extra men. Franz took the wheel, with an armed soldier beside him, and drove down towards the forest.

Our passengers, mostly Resistance members, were a rough and boisterous lot. As might be expected, their language, French, was spiced with a generous sprinkling of slang and profanities. Their spirits seemed undampened despite their arrest and eventual fate. They kept up a continuous flow of chatter among themselves, oblivious to the "German" guards and the nurse, and apparently unconcerned about whether their new captors understood them.

"I wonder where those sons-of-bitches are taking us now?" said one of them to no one in particular.

"One of the guards told me we were being shipped to Germany," replied another voice.

"Germany, my ass. More likely the Gestapo and a firing squad, if we're lucky." This came from one of the younger men.

"Germany. That means the concentration camp. Not a good place to be, gang. Heard some terrible things about them camps. At least here the food wasn't too bad." And so the talk went. Another young tough expressed an interest in assaulting the nurse and was immediately rebuffed by another, who asked how he intended to go about it, there being standing room only for them all. This last remark was met with roars of laughter.

It seemed as if the boys did not have a care in the world. I supposed that they had learned not to think of the morrow, knowing that there might be none. I wondered what they would say when they knew who we were and where they were being taken. As we bounced along they gradually quietened down.

The truck had been rumbling through the forest for almost two hours when it slowed down in a clearing, then came to a halt. The boys looked at each other, suddenly worried. One of them suggested that they had arrived in Germany; but an older man said, no, Germany was further away. Several sounded pessimistic and wondered aloud if this was where they would be machine-gunned and dumped, as had happened to Pierre's group.

At this point one of our soldiers shouted, "Silence!" in French at the top of his lungs. The men were instantly mute, completely baffled. The soldiers yelled, "Allons, les gars, terminus! Tout le monde descend!" (Come on, you guys, last stop! Everyone out!)

One of the youths next to me cried out in excitement, "Nom de Dieu! The Boche talks French, or am I dreaming!"

I had been waiting impatiently for the chance to open my mouth. I interrupted him in French to say that he was not dreaming; then I cried out, "Don't you guys understand French? Out you go! We're not Germans! You're free, you bums! This is a Resistance group!"

When the message had sunk in, their jubilation was spontaneous and completely uninhibited. They embraced each other and the soldiers, they hugged me and shook my hands, and expressed themselves in terse, excited exclamations: "Ça alors, c'est un coup!" "Mais c'est fantastique!" "Incroyable!" "Formidable!" Their joy brought tears to my eyes. I felt as if I had been freed too.

We learned that the extra fifteen prisoners had been jailed for minor offences, such as poaching and black-market dealings. In retrospect, their release to us must have been an oversight on the part of the citadel sergeant or perhaps a misunderstanding of Franz's orders. Anyway, these men were so grateful to be free that they offered then and there to join the maquis. The operation was an unqualified success and earned us high praise from the network chief. His congratulations were succinctly suited to the times—"Good work. Well done, everyone."

One wonders what happened at the citadel when a second truck and another officer called two days later to claim the same prisoners, and what the consequences were when both parties figured out what must have happened. It is even possible that nothing at all happened. Snafus were as common in the Wehrmacht as they have always been in armies. There were more of them than usual at the Gestapo, as I had myself noted time and again, probably because many of the individuals the Gestapo recruited were brutish and stupid characters, a good number of them with criminal backgrounds and low IQs. It was well known, too, that the Wehrmacht wasted no love on the Gestapo, so that when orders from the latter were found to be redundant or forged, or even messed up by the Wehrmacht themselves, they were often conveniently forgotten. We were relieved and not overly surprised, then, that Mueller never did hear about "Operation Citadel".

Our Resistance group could count a number of successful operations to its credit, but while some, like the one at Dinant citadel, saved lives, others lost them. I was involved in one of the latter, in a sortie against the enemy, but only as a witness. Jean had insisted that I go along with him as he felt the experience would nicely round off my instruction in guerrilla warfare.

The operation was an ambush planned in the spring of 1944, and involved some forty or fifty maquisards. A particular stretch of road was to be mined with high explosives in the heart of the forêt de Soignes, some twenty-five kilometres southeast of Brussels. Our objective was to blow up part of a convoy of eight army trucks carrying arms and ammunition, then capture the rest. We were also to shoot any survivors and strip them of their uniforms and identification documents. All such war materials and equipment were sorely needed by the Resistance.

Detailed intelligence information provided us with the convoy's itinerary, the exact time it would take the first truck to reach the mined area, and the approximate strength of the enemy personnel accompanying the convoy. The accuracy of this information was truly amazing, as we were able to appreciate from subsequent events.

Jean, by now well versed in the art of sabotage, had been placed in command and was himself to operate the detonator, which he carried around with him. Since he had to be on the ambush site at around three in the morning, he warned me that I would have to be up very early. Accordingly I was awake and dressed when he came to fetch me at two-thirty.

After a short trip we arrived in the forest, where ghost-like figures were moving about silently in the darkness. Some of the men had been working since midnight, digging up the road, packing it with explosives, and smoothly resurfacing it, while others laid the lines connected to the detonator, which was by now hidden in the woods, well back from the road. Everyone worked in absolute silence, each provided with a tiny flashlight as his only source of light.

In the eerie scene, I was afraid of being lost amid all the activity, so I kept close to Jean. He explained to me how his contraption was supposed to work, but I understood only that the detonator was connected to two separate mines for faster action. Finally he knelt by the plunger and invited me to sit on the ground and watch. He checked the time and whispered, "If my sources are correct, the convoy should be here in a little over ten minutes." The other men had assumed their posts, spread along both sides of the road and hidden behind the trees, their sub-machine-guns at the ready. Although I could not see them against the blackness of the trees, I sensed their presence. Jean carried a Luger pistol himself.

Time passed in slow motion. In the oppressive silence, I felt vaguely worried about the outcome, wondering whether everything would work out as planned or end in disaster. But as I had never witnessed carnage before, I cannot say I was shaking with fear. The first light of day filtered gradually through the foliage, and I could now discern the road ahead, partly obscured by the trees. The birds around us began their chirping, and I welcomed the inappropriately cheerful noise. The sounds reinforced my confidence in survival.

Pre-arranged whistles warned us that the convoy had been sighted. Soon after we could hear the distant rumble and see the powerful headlight beams that heralded the approach of the leading truck. The moment it entered the mined area, Jean depressed the plunger, and the vehicle instantly disintegrated with a deafening explosion of debris in all directions. I remember watching a hand detached from its body land on the ground a few feet away from us. A ghoulish sight.

Jean sharply depressed the plunger a second time, and the second truck exploded. As a result of the shock and the sudden intense heat, the ammunition stores of the first two trucks ignited the third vehicle. Jean and I flattened ourselves against the ground behind a tree, as projectiles from the wrecks popped and crackled and whizzed all around us in a grisly travesty of a fireworks display. Half a body, legless, soared through the air and disappeared into the treetops.

I lay as if hypnotized, watching the gruesome spectacle as the rat-tat-tat of Schmeissers and Sten guns rang in my ears. The German soldiers not blown to bits by the explosions had jumped free of the trucks and scattered, some shooting at shadows, others fleeing in panic. To the last man they were mowed down by the Resistance guerrillas who had been lying in wait for them. After an endless time, the firing lessened, then died, leaving only the crackling sounds of the burning vehicles and the occasional shouts of our men echoing in the suddenly quiet forest.

I got up, took a few cautious steps, and looked around. Nearby I saw a body writhing on the ground; it was a wounded German soldier, gesturing for help. I was surprised to see that he was not a young

man, and I pitied him lying there, begging for his life. My wartime
rancour forgotten for the moment, I called to Jean. He came over with
one of our men. I asked if we could do anything to save the man. He
said no, then gave an order to his subordinate: "Finish him off."

I understood that neither Jean nor his colleague was heartless or
cruel, though the episode depressed me. Afterwards Jean explained to
me that rescuing the soldier or any of his fellows would have endangered the whole operation. We could not have passed them on to the
care of ambulances and hospital facilities, as a regular army unit could
have done. This immediate execution of the survivors, he said, was
really the humane thing to do, kinder than sparing them and letting
them die a slower and more painful death later.

The macabre task of stripping the dead bodies remained. Our men
removed everything down to the soldiers' identity tags. Finally only
the stark naked corpses remained, lying on the ground where they had
fallen.

Five trucks had remained intact. They were quickly boarded and
driven away by the guerrillas, dressed as Wehrmacht soldiers. Each
followed a different trail and all of them reached camp safely. We left
the other vehicles ablaze; luckily the absence of wind and the width of
the road prevented the fire from spreading into the surrounding forest. The operation had yielded a welcome quantity of arms, ammunition, uniforms, and identification documents, as well as the five trucks,
without a single casualty on our side.

My own feelings about the adventure were ambivalent. While I was
glad to have survived, and proud, in an impersonal sort of way, of the
losses the Resistance had inflicted on the enemy, I was also chastened
by my first experience of war at close quarters. In particular I remembered the lone soldier who had begged for his life and had been
"finished off" instead. I had to remind myself that Hitler's war was
not a gentleman's war, and it was his kind of war we were fighting.

15

From High Above

The leitmotiv of the spring of 1944, as it is fixed in my memory, was the distant overhead drone of masses of Allied bombers on their way to Germany, day after day and night after night. Even after forty years, I associate the memory of that sound with moments of intense feelings, when fear, hope, anxiety, and relief followed one another in lightning succession, all in the space of a few minutes, or hours, or even days. The sound filled my heart with hope and an increasing certainty of the final victory.

However, I was unable to foresee or even imagine my own involvement with the crew of a British bomber in that spring of 1944. Franz brought the news to me early one Tuesday morning, just after my landlady had left for work. A British bomber had been shot down the previous night, just outside Uccle, an upper-middle-class suburb of Brussels. Out of a crew of nine, six surviving airmen had bailed out of the plane and parachuted onto the grounds of a huge private estate in the district. In this they were lucky, for the owner of the grounds and adjoining villa happened to be a staunch patriot, whose son had joined the underground and knew Jean well. The owner had gathered the six men, one of them with a fractured arm, into his villa, where he had attended to their needs and provided them with civilian clothes from his large wardrobe. But he advised them that they would have to be moved to a safer place before daybreak. The Germans usually had a fairly accurate idea of the area in which parachutists landed after a plane had been shot down. He expected they would begin to comb the neighbourhood at the crack of dawn, if not earlier, looking for survivors, and his premises were sure to be searched.

His son was summoned, and he drove the six men to a temporary hide-out, the small apartment of another Resistance member's sister. The place was not really large enough to accommodate all six men, and extra space was urgently needed for three of them. The son phoned Jean for help, and Jean, in turn, contacted Franz.

That was why Franz came to see me that morning. He wondered if I would be willing to put up the three airmen in my room for a couple of days, while arrangements were made for their transportation to a maquis camp. He stressed that my place, small though it might be, was the only safe one he could think of in Brussels at the moment. He may well have been right, for we knew that several underground people connected with escape routes for Allied airmen had been arrested of late.

My room, as I have said, was tiny, about nine feet by twelve feet, with hardly enough space for one person, let alone four. A second difficulty would be Mme de Bruyn, whose bedroom was next to mine, and who could not know of the three men's presence there. The arrangement seemed impossible, but time was short, so I asked Franz to bring them along before Mme de Bruyn returned from work.

He was back with my three guests just before noon. All were men in their early twenties, and unmistakably British in appearance. They exuded an air of what we in Belgium called "le flegme anglais"—a quiet confidence, despite their present danger. I did not speak a word of English at the time, and only one of them spoke a few words of French, but somehow we managed to communicate and get organized. Franz had provided a basketful of canned goods. Without real cooking facilities in my room, my guests had to eat straight from the cans. At night two of them shared my bed while the third took his turn on watch at the window. If he heard or saw anything unusual, he was to let me know. In case of alert, they were to hide in the attic.

I had to sleep on the floor, with a rug for a mattress and a coat for a blanket. I did not sleep much, however, for fear of being discovered by my landlady. With only a thin wall between our room and hers, we had to be absolutely silent during the night. No whispering was allowed, nor moving around, nor snoring. As they were not allowed to make use of the bathroom out on the landing, a chamber-pot was provided for their minor calls of nature.

All three men behaved with impeccable decorum throughout their stay. From the one who spoke a little French, I gathered that they had been on three previous raids over Germany before they were brought down. More than that I did not have the chance to find out. On the second day Franz called to replenish our provisions and to advise us that transportation would not be available for another day or two. He said that the Germans were still hunting for the missing airmen and checking cars and trucks at random. So my guests stayed on. In our cramped conditions, we were not cheered by the news, but my accustomed good fortune held.

On Thursday morning, Mme de Bruyn apologetically informed me that she would be away for the weekend, starting Friday. She had to accompany her employer, an elderly semi-invalid woman, to Mons, and would not be back until Sunday evening. She hoped I would not mind too much staying in the house all by myself. I assured her that I would be fine. Had the poor woman known the truth, she would have fainted.

When Franz heard the news later that day, his reaction was unexpected and immediate. The three remaining airmen had to leave the other apartment right away. They had been spotted by some suspicious neighbours and were in imminent danger of being arrested. I was speechless. "After all," he continued, "now that you have the whole place at your disposal, there's no reason why I couldn't bring the other chaps over here, too." I made him promise that they would be gone by Sunday afternoon.

And so on Friday three more airmen arrived, including the one with his arm in a sling. And now they had the run of the house. They could talk freely, stretch their legs at will, sink comfortably into the armchairs, lie on the sofa, and use the bathroom without problems. Their reactions amused and delighted me. They behaved almost like happy children on holiday. To celebrate I even lit Mme de Bruyn's coal stove and cooked a hot meal for them all. On Saturday one of them volunteered to cook dinner, and we were all pleased to find his efforts very palatable. By that night the boys had scrubbed the kitchen clean, polished the coal stove, and put everything back in place, leaving the rooms even cleaner than they had been before their arrival. On Sunday afternoon they departed in three different vehicles, after saying goodbye to me with fervent thanks and warm handshakes. All seven of us felt as if we had been hostess and guests for several weeks, instead of just a few days. Via the underground I later learned that all six had reached Spain safely and from there had found their way back to England. At least that was what I was told. I admit that today I cannot even remember their first names.

On Sunday night my landlady returned from her brief trip. When she entered the house she exclaimed happily, "Why, Madame Andrée, you have even polished my stove! That's hard work! You shouldn't have done it!" I told her cheerfully that I hadn't minded at all.

The good woman never learned about those five disruptive days, not even after the Liberation. She would surely have misconstrued the whole episode if I had tried to tell her. She was convinced that Franz, Jean, and any other Resistance characters who occasionally happened to drop in were all lovers of mine. But I never bore her a grudge for suspecting me of being a loose woman, unfaithful to my prisoner-of-war husband.

This was not, however, my first encounter with the Allied air forces. Almost a year earlier, in January 1943, I had arrived at Gestapo head-quarters one Wednesday morning to find two guards on duty outside Mueller's office door. Intrigued, I asked why they were there. They answered that there was a VIP meeting in progress inside. I supposed this meant that some SS generals or other high-ranking officers were involved. My curiosity satisfied, I went on to my office.

Franz, who was away on some mission, had asked me to sort out some papers for him for his return. While I was doing so, I heard a strange loud noise, which I could not identify. It was rather like the drone of a huge motor, but the sound seemed distorted by its nearness. It definitely came from the direction of the street. Our office window faced the back, so I ran out towards the front-facing window at the end of the hall.

To my amazement the window was completely obscured by what looked like the fuselage of a plane floating before my eyes right at window level. Simultaneously I heard what sounded like the sharp staccato of a powerful machine-gun firing, and I rushed back to my office to duck under a table, sure that this was the prelude to a bombing attack. But the splutter of the machine-gun stopped, leaving a deathly silence throughout the building. Although the raid seemed to have lasted much longer, it was all over in a minute or two. I waited a few minutes; then, hearing a growing commotion in the hall, I pulled myself together and decided to see what it was all about.

There were soldiers everywhere, some carrying white sheets, some with stretchers and others with first-aid kits. The guards were gone. Mueller's office door stood wide open. Inside I saw overturned chairs, motionless bodies on the floor, broken glass, and an unbelievable amount of blood everywhere.

Mueller walked out slowly, his left arm soaked in blood. When I approached him to ask about the raid, he impatiently shooed me away. "Don't worry. I'm all right. Go back to work."

It did not take a genius to piece together what had happened. The plane I had seen a few moments before had skilfully flown on a level with the top floor just long enough to allow the pilot or his assistant to fire directly through the window of Mueller's office. The results impressed me as evidence of remarkably accurate shooting, or, at the least, great luck. I assumed that the pilot and his plane had escaped unharmed.

After all the excitement, I needed some fresh air. I put away my papers and closed the office. I emerged from the building to find that a crowd had assembled across the street. Naturally, half the bystanders had no idea what was going on. Others who had witnessed the raid were eagerly discussing it with their neighbours. I spoke to one person who had watched the whole thing.

According to that witness, the plane had appeared from nowhere, flying at low level, and sprayed the Gestapo building, at the same time hitting the anti-aircraft crew on the roof, who must have been caught unprepared. Then it had swung away, flying low for a short while, almost touching the treetops along avenue Louise, and dropping several dozen small Belgian flags before roaring away. Franz later confirmed that one of the anti-aircraft guns had been hit and two of the gunners killed in the raid.

Gestapo guards now came out in force to disperse the crowd. They arrested a number of bystanders, whether merely to extract first-hand information or in spiteful reprisal for the attack, I do not know.

Weeks later more of the story was supplied by Resistance intelligence. It seemed to confirm, at least in part, what the first-hand witness had told me. A Belgian pilot, a member of the British forces, had, without permission from his superiors, flown his Typhoon all the way to Brussels from England; he had apparently returned to his base safely, with his aircraft intact. Despite his obvious breach of discipline, this young man had undertaken a bold and amazing mission, calculated and executed with supreme skill and audacity, a unique feat in the annals of the war.

Franz and I knew that several high-ranking Gestapo and SS officers, as well as many others on the lower floors, had been killed in that raid, for the pilot had thoroughly peppered the whole building. However, we wondered whether he had also known there was a meeting of SS and Gestapo VIPs that day and in that particular office. It remained a complete mystery to me until recently, when I obtained additional information from Charles Demoulin, author of *Mes Oiseaux de Feux* and a former comrade-in-arms and close companion of the pilot. It appears that the latter, a Belgian flying officer named Jean-Michel de Selys-Longchamps, had been completely unaware of that meeting. It was simply a fluke.

This feat, for which the pilot—killed in action later that year—was awarded the Distinguished Flying Cross, is commemorated today by a plaque on the former Gestapo building, 453 avenue Louise. Translated from the French, the plaque reads:

"In broad daylight,
on 20 January 1943,
this building, occupied by the Gestapo
during the 1940–45 war,
sustained vengeful fire from the guns of a plane piloted by
Capitaine Baron Jean-Michel
de SELYS-LONGCHAMPS
of the 1ᵉʳ Régiment de Guides,
Flying Officer in the ROYAL AIR FORCE."

16

Through the Roof

The world within a world that made up the Resistance contained a great diversity of tradesmen and professionals who provided a pool of invaluable expertise in our struggle. Of particular value were members like Jean, men of many accomplishments, great resourcefulness, and unshakeable loyalty. One of his skills was a working knowledge of wireless radio operation, acquired as a radio ham operator before the war. Inevitably, then, one of his many duties in the underground included that of radio operator.

By 1944 an increasing number of German radio-detector vans were cruising the streets, and a radio operator and his set were in constant danger of being discovered. Those same vans, however, had a much harder time pinpointing the exact locations of transmitters operating within the heart of the city, where there was plenty of interference from motors, trolley-cars, and other sources of electrical currents.

A few months earlier Jean had discovered such a choice location, when a house on rue Dautzenberg was vacated and offered to the underground for an indefinite length of time. He installed his set in the cellar and established regular contact with London, steadily receiving and transmitting messages for three solid months without a hitch.

One day in late March 1944 I met Jean by chance on the street. We had walked along together for a while, exchanging the latest news, when he asked if I had the afternoon free. I replied yes, and why?

"I thought you might be interested in seeing how we contact London."

"It would be interesting, but is it really safe? This is no time for me to get caught."

"I've been operating from the same place for the last three months, several times a week. Why should we get caught today of all days? Of course it's safe." I was somewhat surprised that the address was a mere stone's throw from the Gestapo. Then I decided that it would probably be safer there than farther away. I accepted the invitation, on condition that I be able to leave sharply at four.

"Fine. I'm having two trainees in with us this afternoon. We'll pick them up after lunch and go straight over."

Rue Dautzenberg is a relatively short street that climbs its way towards avenue Louise, which it intersects. The vacant house, a sturdy, two-storey Victorian structure with solid oak doors, stood about a hundred feet from the corner of that intersection. We arrived there about two o'clock, after parking Jean's truck far down the street. For the next couple of hours the boys busied themselves with transmitting and receiving the signals, which I found quite exciting, though they were all in code. Jean told me that from the general tone of the messages received lately, he had a feeling that some big military operation was about to begin, but he had no idea where or just when. The Allied landing of June 6, 1944, in Normandy, a little over two months later, proved that his hunch was correct.

I looked at my watch at five minutes to four, just as I thought I heard a knock at the front door. This was followed by several louder knocks, which alerted us all. At that point I remembered having noticed a narrow strip of daylight that filtered through the uppermost part of the cellar window. I climbed up on a stool and stood on tiptoe to look through the slit. All I could see were the distinctive heels, soles, and uppers of jackboots, and it was not hard for me to guess who wore them. I called out, in a frantic whisper, "Les Boches sont là!" There was a moment of stunned silence, and then Jean took charge. While the Germans banged harder on the door, yelling, "Aufmachen!" he ordered that the transmitter be left open, so that London would know something had gone wrong; then he swiftly led the way upstairs to the attic. The Boches were now trying to break down the massive door with their rifle butts. Just as we reached the attic, they fired at the lock, the door itself still holding firm.

Like most European attics, this one had a small skylight that opened upwards and out over the slope of a steeply pitched roof covered with red tiles. One by one we climbed through the hatch, trying to get a firm grip on the ridge without dislodging the tiles. Had they crashed onto the street below, they would have given away our escape and our route. Jean closed the skylight after us without locking it, to allow for possible re-entry later. He quietly told me to go left, while he and his companions would go to the right. We wished each other good luck, knowing full well that if any of the Gestapo men happened to open the skylight and look out, we would have had it. We had to move away quickly and surely over the steep slopes without sliding down and breaking our necks on the pavement below or, worse, falling into the hands of our pursuers.

I found very soon that the only safe way to move was by heaving myself up to the ridge and, lying flat on my stomach with legs astride to avoid rolling off, crawling forward in snake-like fashion. The rough edges of the clay tiles bit deeply into my chest and scratched my thighs, causing excruciating pain and slowing my progress, as I had to stop to rest every few feet.

The neighbouring roofs were flush with the first, so that I was able to advance, slowly and painfully, from one ridge to the next. As I crept, I watched for an open skylight where I might crawl in unnoticed. All the ones I could see were closed. There was no turning back. I soon lost track of the number I had passed, and I realized that had I wished to return to my original escape hatch, I would not have known which one it was, since they all looked alike. Painfully and slowly I continued to crawl until I reached the end of the last roof facing rue Dautzenberg.

The ridge level of the next row of houses facing avenue Louise was some three or four feet lower than my present perch. My watch now showed quarter past six and dusk was closing in. I had been struggling along for two interminable hours. I was exhausted, cold, hungry, and thoroughly miserable. And I had to make a cruel choice: either to remain in that ridiculously painful position until morning, which seemed unbearable, or to make a supreme effort and jump onto the lower ridge. After several further minutes of weighing my options, I braced myself and jumped forward, falling awkwardly astride the lower ridge. The leap added more scrapes and scratches, but I was still in one piece, so I soon resumed my agonizing progress, not knowing what was to happen to me next.

I had passed two more windows that were hermetically sealed when

I glimpsed, in the growing darkness, an open skylight ahead. Without any further thought, I slid and turned and wriggled my way inside it until I found myself hanging, feet down, and gripping the narrow window-ledge with my hands. The attic inside was pitch dark and I could distinguish nothing. I could only let go and hope for an easy landing.

Instead I crashed to the floor, which was farther away than I had calculated. The immediate searing pain in my ankle was the last straw. Miserable and lost and now incapacitated with a sprained ankle in a strange house, I remained crumpled where I had landed and cried like a baby. I did not care any more what would happen to me.

After a few minutes I heard the footsteps of someone coming slowly up the stairs. A door creaked open and I was suddenly blinded by a flashlight beam shining in my face. When the glare shifted away from my eyes, a dim light shone through the open door, revealing an older woman who stood there peering at me. Finally she spoke: "What in heaven's name are you doing here? How did you get up here?"

I answered feebly, "I jumped through the open skylight. Ran away from the Germans. If you're pro-German, go ahead, hand me over to them. I don't care." This was one of the rare moments during the war when I completely lost my spirit.

To my surprise the woman's voice was kindly. "My child, I am no friend of the Germans, believe me. First of all, let's get out of here. Follow me downstairs."

"I'm sorry, I can't walk. I sprained my ankle when I jumped."

She helped me up and gently supported and guided me as I hobbled down the narrow wooden steps and into her living room, which seemed immense. I sank into the nearest armchair, utterly drained. My hostess, whose name I am ashamed to have forgotten, was truly kind and charitable. She insisted on bandaging my ankle and talked as she did so, telling me that she had thought she was going to catch a burglar in the attic. At first she imagined that the noise had come from the cellar. It was her servant's day off, she said, and the careless girl had forgotten to close the skylight after cleaning the attic. I gave a sigh and said it had been really lucky for me. Then I told her I worked for the Resistance, but was not allowed to say any more.

"I understand. I have two sons in the forces in England myself. Haven't heard from them in a long time, though." The houses on both sides of the street were full of German officers, she informed me, and I had been lucky to fall into hers, especially on the very day when her servant was away. She thought it a miracle, and I could only agree.

After sharing a substantial and delicious meal with me, she would not hear of my leaving. She told me that I was in no condition to walk and that she would not let me go until I was fully recovered. Besides, she had already prepared the guest room for me. I was completely overwhelmed and could not express my gratitude adequately. The good lady added, in a confidential tone, "I'll tell the servant that you are a niece of mine on a visit, and that you sprained your ankle falling down the stairs. You know how servants talk. The less you tell them, the better."

Until my rescue I had been preoccupied with my own survival. Now I had time to fret about Jean and his companions. Might the Gestapo men have followed them over the roof? What then? It was too late in the evening to try to contact Jean or Franz, but I promised myself I would make some phone calls in the morning.

I rang up Jean's place early the next day, but there was no answer. I imagined him shot or arrested, and in a panic, I quickly rang Franz's apartment. He answered immediately and seemed relieved to hear my voice. I told him I was safe, but would be away a few days because of my ankle.

The news of Jean was good. He and his friends had hid on the roofs until dark, then had come back through the same skylight when they were sure that the house was empty. They had left safely through the front door and driven away in Jean's truck.

When I recounted my own adventure and miraculous rescue, Franz, suddenly recovered from his earlier anxiety, gave me hell for taking unwarranted risks. He demanded to know where I was staying. I replied somewhere on the avenue Louise, but refused to give him the number. I realized I was distrusting him again, and he found me very stubborn at such times.

A similar situation had arisen a few weeks earlier, when he had ordered me to do a night job at Evere airport, in a distant suburb northeast of Brussels. The airport had been turned into a German military air base during the Occupation, and it also contained a large ammunition dump. My job would have been to divert the sentry's attention while Resistance men sneaked through to do sabotage work there. I had instinctively refused to go although I could not give him a satisfactory excuse at the time. Finally, much exasperated, he had given me a final order to do as I was told. But I still did not go.

On the night of that mission, a massive Allied air raid struck the base, scoring direct hits on aircraft, personnel, and the ammunition dump, which nearly destroyed everything else as it went up. There were many casualties, including the sentry on duty and some of the Resistance people of that group. Had I done as I was told, I would almost certainly have been one of the casualties.

When Franz saw me the following day, he said, with an indifferent expression on his face, that he was glad to find me alive and well. But I have always wondered whether he had known, through London, that an air raid was scheduled that night, and had hoped to get rid of me. I mused that perhaps, as a Jewish girl, I had become too much of a liability to him. I certainly felt I had to be on my guard from then on.

I stayed at my benefactress's home for three blissful days, during which I was nursed, fed, and treated like a princess. To find a sympathetic soul in the midst of so much greed and ugliness was a balm to my sagging spirits. The enforced idleness also gave me time to brood on the strained and unusual circumstances of my life over the previous few years, and on the uncertainty of my future.

At least my work as governess at the Herrandts', five days a week from nine to six, provided me with a small salary and a semblance of normality, as well as a substantial lunch. The rest of the time I had to fend for myself, trying to stave off hunger. I thought about the role I had to play at the Gestapo, maintaining my uncomfortable connection with Franz and occasionally taking part in some Resistance operation. I knew these assignments often obliged me to be absent too long from my paying work, my only means of support, but the Resistance expected total commitment from its members. If any individual chose to quit, he or she was treated like all army deserters in times of war: when caught, they were tried, and often shot.

If I had chosen to give up my clandestine activities and gone into hiding—an alternative about which I sometimes fantasized when feeling low—I would have betrayed not only the Resistance but also my own conscience and deepest convictions. So I kept going, struggling all the time, living with an undercurrent of chronic anxiety: fear of losing my job; fear of being picked up in the street and sent to Germany for forced labour (I could not always carry my German ID, and my Belgian one would not have saved me); fear of being recognized by some outside acquaintance while at the Gestapo, or of being reported, or otherwise uncovered, and arrested. And I was haunted by the fear that I might never see my parents again, or my husband.

Despite the comfort and safety of my refuge on avenue Louise, my old restlessness returned on the third day of my stay there. I longed to get out again and bury my worries in action. I let my hostess know that, much to my regret, I would have to leave. When she saw me off at the door, she wished me luck with tears in her eyes. She told me that I could stay at her home whenever and for as long as I wished. I thanked her for everything and then clasped her in my arms, crying. It was an emotional departure.

After the Liberation, I paid my generous hostess a surprise visit. I gave her the bouquet of flowers I had brought and warmly thanked her again for her timely hospitality. She was delighted and naturally astonished to see me. Over coffee and cake, she told me she had not believed that I would survive the rigours of underground warfare, and she confessed she had given me up for dead. I learned that her sons were alive and well and still in England. I felt happy for her and wished her well with all my heart.

I now felt reasonably fit again, except for a slight limp, and decided it was time to show my face at the Gestapo office. Frau Bertha, always eager to find work for me, greeted me with a stack of the unending paperwork to sort and take to the chief's office. When Mueller saw me limping, he showed concern. I dismissed it as nothing serious. I said I had fallen down some stairs and sprained my ankle, but I was all right now.

While I spoke, my eyes fell on Jean's now familiar transmitter, sitting on his late assistant's desk. Mueller followed my surprised gaze and, being evidently in one of his more expansive moods, commented on it. "That transmitter was brought in a few days ago. Would you believe we found it operating almost under our very noses? Open, and still warm when it was picked up!"

Some devilish impulse made me say: "How wonderful! So you arrested the operator, too!"

His self-satisfaction dimmed noticeably. "Well, no. Unfortunately, there was no one there."

"But didn't you say the transmitter was still open and warm? Surely the operator couldn't have been far away?"

The colonel shifted slightly in his chair and sighed. "The men said there was nobody in the house."

"Oh! It was a house. I hope they searched it thoroughly. You know, Herr Mueller, there are a lot of nooks and crannies where one can hide in a house. Even the backyard. Or the attic."

Mueller, as if struck by a new idea, brightened and looked at me appreciatively. "You know, Fräulein Olga, you have a good point there. I hadn't thought of it. Let's call the men and hear what they have to say. Don't go. I want you to be present."

The henchmen were summoned, and soon all three entered, saluted, and stood stiffly at attention. The colonel addressed them smoothly. "When you confiscated the transmitter from the Dautzenbergstrasse house, and saw no one around, did you search the house?"

The officer in charge answered crisply, "Ja, Herr Oberst, but there was nobody there."

"And you looked upstairs?"

"Ja, Herr Oberst, but we found nobody."

With the chief's permission, I could not resist asking a few questions myself. "Did you look behind the house? In the backyard?"

"The back door was locked from inside, Fräulein."

"Did you search the attic?"

"No, Fräulein."

"Oh? Why not?"

"We listened for any noise there, but it was quiet, so there could not have been anyone there. We would have heard them."

I laughed. "Evidently anyone hiding in the attic would be careful not to make any noise, don't you think?"

The man stood there helplessly, not knowing what to say, as Mueller's face turned a rich crimson.

Then he exploded, heaping caustic insults on his men for their sloppy work. He ended by sentencing them all to six days in prison: "And after that I'll see what to do with you! Raus!"

When the subordinates were gone, Mueller turned to me, apologizing as if he had somehow disappointed me: "Why did I not think of this myself? But, you know, Fräulein Olga, I have so many things on my mind. Too much to do," he said, shaking his head wearily. I sympathized and said of course, Herr Mueller, of course.

I contemplated the punishment of the three Gestapo men with a perverse satisfaction. Their negligence had saved our lives and enhanced my position with Mueller, as well as compensating to some extent, I felt, for all the suffering I had endured on account of that transmitter.

Mueller invited me to join him for a cup of coffee at the Café Louise, where we had first met. Over our steaming cups, he became confidential, complaining about the vast responsibilities heaped on his shoulders and about his need for some intelligent assistant—like me, for instance. I anticipated the coming proposal: "By the way, how is your health these days? Think you could do a little more work now?"

I said I regretted deeply that my heart was still very weak, and that I still needed peace and quiet, and regular medical attention. I was afraid that for some time to come, I would have to continue to restrict my work to a minimum.

Mueller did not press further but talked about Franz, and asked me if something was troubling him lately. "To be quite frank," he said, "I find he is not working as well as he used to. I must say I am rather disappointed in him. He had better pull up his socks."

I said I had noticed myself that he had seemed slightly depressed lately, but added that I was sure he would get over it soon and be himself again. I promised to speak to him. Although our little chat was friendly enough, I did not feel comfortable as I walked back to the office. I resolved to talk with Franz as soon as I could.

Mueller's complaint about his diminishing productivity was a very serious matter. I saw Franz's dilemma as a chronic and nightmarish problem for him. He had to live with the occasional need to sacrifice a few human beings in order to protect his Gestapo cover, which allowed him to save many others. It was a soul-destroying choice, and one that anyone infiltrating the Gestapo faced in the line of duty.

It was difficult to gauge Franz's reaction to my news. He did not confide in me, so that apart from those missions on which we worked together, I knew nothing of his outside activities. I only felt that my decision to be wary of him was further justified.

17

The Führer's
Birthday

April of 1944 is a month I remember mainly because of two events. The first of these was my sheltering of the six British airmen. The second was an unusual birthday party.

Franz received an official invitation that month for both of us, to a reception "in honour of the Führer's birthday". The occasion was sponsored by the top officials of the German forces of occupation in Brussels for April 20, Hitler's birthday, at a hotel on boulevard Anspach. If I had known then that I would write these memoirs forty years later, I would have noted the name of that hotel. It was not one of the internationally known ones, like the Palace or the Metropole. It had been chosen, I remember, because of its immense banquet hall and its first-class catering facilities.

We immediately passed the information on to the underground. The Resistance did not consider carrying out any spectacular plan, such as blowing up the place during the festivities, for this would also have caused the death of a number of innocent hotel guests, as well as the shooting of innumerable hostages and probably other grisly reprisals. However, since the maquis was chronically short of arms, this seemed to be a good opportunity to quietly appropriate a few German service revolvers.

The accepted code of military etiquette—in Germany and many

other nations—requires officers attending any function at which ladies are present to remove their holsters and side-arms as well as the belts to which they are fastened. These are usually left in a secure place on arrival, each guest retrieving his own piece as he leaves.

The underground accordingly conceived an ingenious scheme. The ranks of the Resistance included a large number of professional waiters, most of whom lost no time in applying for the chance to work at the illustrious birthday party. The maître d'hôtel had his own pool of some twelve waiters, but as he needed extra help, he gladly hired another eight from among the applicants—all of whom, unknown to him, happened to belong to the Resistance. Each of these was entrusted with the mission of stealing two guns, a total of sixteen for the eight men. How they were to accomplish this was not revealed, but they claimed to have a well-organized plan.

In our role as faithful supporters of the Reich, Franz and I were obliged to attend the gala. Formal attire was understandably de rigueur. As I certainly could not afford the cost of an evening gown or a decent hairdo, I gave Franz an ultimatum: unless I was enabled to look presentable, he would have to leave me behind. This posed a challenge to him, as he was supposed to be my official escort as well as my fiancé. Typically, he found a clever way of solving the problem without incurring any expense to himself. He sent me to Jean's hairdresser friend, who not only fixed my hair beautifully but provided me with an expensive evening gown, all for the love of country and free of charge.

The party was indeed a lavish affair. My first impression on arrival was of a brightly illuminated and very grand spectacle, in sharp contrast to the dreariness of the occupied city. The reception hall was packed with high-ranking officers from every service: the Wehrmacht, the SS, the Gestapo, the Feldpolizei, and others, interspersed with a few dozen Blitzmädchen trying unsuccessfully to look attractive in their drab grey uniforms. In all, there were some 250 guests, including several prominent Belgian collaborators, whose names we were unfortunately unable to obtain in full during the course of the evening.

The buffet particularly impressed me. It was spread along both sides of the hall's far corner, long tables laden with a vast assortment of the most sumptuous foods, such as I had not seen for four long, lean war years. Russian caviar consorted with smoked salmon; pâté de foie gras de Strasbourg sat beside fish in aspic; colourful plates of wurst and cold cuts lay at the foot of mountains of sliced pumpernickel, white, and rye breads. There were dozens of cheeses, including

my almost forgotten favourites—Brie, Edam, and Emmenthal—and
an enormous baron of beef, presided over by a proud chef, knife in
hand, ready to slice to your order. Topping it all was a collection of
rich, flaky Belgian pies and pastries that I had nearly forgotten existed.

The sight of all these delicacies was more than my starved taste-
buds could stand. At the first opportunity, and every five minutes
thereafter, I made my way through the crowds to the buffet and
stuffed myself until Franz impatiently dragged me away, grumbling
that I was overeating and would make myself sick. It was all very well
for him to preach; I was sure he had never suffered hunger in his life.

The waiters quietly circulated through the crowd like anonymous
black-and-white robots, their trays loaded with glasses of champagne.
As agents on the job, Franz and I were not supposed to drink, though
I was allowed one single glass of champagne. Later Franz refilled my
glass with clear water. At the other end of the hall, near the pantry
and kitchens, a long table had been provided for the officers' belts and
loaded holsters.

After a general toast and the inevitable "Heil Hitler" to the
Führer's portrait hanging on the wall above us, the military orchestra
played the German national anthem and followed up with a familiar
medley of rousing German waltzes and marches. Franz was a poor
and reluctant dancer and so left me at the mercy of whoever decided
to partner me.

During one waltz, I noticed Mueller standing in a corner alone and
apparently brooding. After the dance I went over to him, pretending
to pay my respects. I asked why he was not dancing. He replied with a
frown that he was not in the mood, as he had just received bad news
from home. I offered my condolences and asked what had happened.
His home in Germany had been bombed and razed. Fortunately his
wife and daughter had been away at the time, he said, adding a few
curses against the Engländer to blame. I uttered the usual platitudes
and gracefully took my leave of him, privately thanking heaven for
this bit of justice. Certainly the news of Mueller's misfortune did not
deter me from revisiting the buffet and helping myself to another
mouthful of wurst.

Around eleven-thirty Franz and I were thinking of leaving, when
the music suddenly stopped. All eyes turned towards the bandstand
where Mueller stood calling for silence. He spoke crisply, once more
the Gestapo hound: "Meine Damen und Herren, I regret that I must
ask everyone to stay on. It appears that some pistols are missing. Will
all officers please check their holsters and report to me if any of their

side-arms are missing. All the exits are guarded and no one will be allowed to leave until further orders. Thank you."

I glanced sideways at my partner, and Franz returned the look. Our black-and-white robots had done their work well. Mueller beckoned to Franz and he obediently left me.

In total fifteen revolvers were reported missing. Mueller ordered Franz and another Gestapo officer to check all the hotel guests and search their rooms. In a little less than an hour they were back, having found nothing. Only then did Mueller think of summoning the French-speaking maître d'. Using Franz as his interpreter, he questioned him. "Do you know all the men who work for you? How many do you have here tonight?"

The maître d' stood shaking in his patent-leather shoes. "I can guarantee my own men's integrity, all twelve of them. But there are, of course, the eight extras, though I hired only those with the very best references."

"Bring them all in here and line them up. I want to see them all, immediately." The headwaiter rushed off and called all his staff to report to him, forthwith, in the hall. They arrived on the double and lined up as directed. Mueller started counting, counted again, then said, "You told me there were twenty men in all. I find only twelve. Where are the others?"

"I'll get them right away, sir." The poor man was off again, searching high and low for the missing extras. No one had seen them leave and they were nowhere to be found. He reported back, spreading his arms in a gesture of helplessness.

Mueller's face hardened. "If these men were not seen leaving through either the front or the back door, they must have found another exit somewhere. Is there another exit from the hotel?"

The maître d' thought for a moment, then seemed to remember. "Of course there is the wine cellar door, but it has been condemned and is always padlocked."

"We shall go down to the wine cellar then, and see." The wine cellar door was indeed closed but the padlock was broken. The door opened into a dark, deserted back alley. Mueller remarked unnecessarily, "So this is how they left." To the maître d', he added, "I suppose you took their names, addresses, and identity numbers? I want to see them at once."

"Certainly, sir. Right away."

The Resistance had its guns. At the height of the party, the extras had inconspicuously sneaked away one by one, each with his booty, through the cellar door and into a waiting truck in the back alley. To cover their escape, the driver had kept his sub-machine-gun handy. By eleven o'clock they had all slipped away.

Mueller's request for the waiters' names and addresses was an exercise in futility, for surely he must have expected all the agents' papers to be fake. He told Franz himself that the arms theft was the work of the Resistance. But he had to save face before the "distinguished" guests.

He slowly mounted the bandstand once more and announced, with a show of authority, "We know who is responsible for stealing the revolvers. They will be arrested and punished. Ladies and gentlemen, you may go now. Good night." It was exactly two-thirty in the morning. I had spent most of the waiting time obsessively nibbling away at the buffet goodies. I felt bloated.

One thing bothered me about the operation, and I asked Franz about it later. "What about these men's pay? Obviously they weren't paid for their work as waiters at the hotel."

Franz laughed. "Don't worry about that. Those guys paid themselves generously. Together with the guns, they carried away some of the cellar's best vintage wines." We never learned the fate of the maître d'.

Despite the incident of the missing revolvers, the officers and other Nazi guests present at the party had not shown signs of being down-hearted or pessimistic about the outcome of the war; on the contrary, they had seemed to hold firmly to the belief that the Führer and his armies would lead them to victory. They could not have known that the public celebration of Hitler's birthday, in Brussels and elsewhere on that day in April 1944, would be his last one, and that he would spend his next birthday hidden in a bunker under the Reichstag, a few days before his ignominious death at his own hands.

They certainly did not know, nor did we at the time, that D-Day was just two months away, leading eventually to the downfall of the Third Reich. Nor could we guess then that Brussels would be liberated in a mere five months' time.

18

Gnawing Doubts

Towards the end of May 1944 I found myself in St-Pierre hospital for an appendectomy. The operation led to some minor complications, so I rested there for a couple of weeks. The Gestapo made daily rounds looking for Jewish patients in the hospitals. If discovered, these people were immediately seized and carted away—whether on the operating table, in intensive care, or convalescing—to be deported and murdered cruelly and slowly, assuming they survived removal from the hospital. Fortunately, since I was registered as Andrée Fiévez, the Gestapo that patrolled the hospital belonged to another section, independent from the avenue Louise headquarters. In retrospect, I realize that Hitler, in his obsession with the Jews, blindly squandered a sizeable and much-needed share of his manpower and equipment on hunting them down and persecuting them—even the sick at hospitals —at a time when he should have mustered the totality of his dwindling manpower and matériel to defend his thousand-year Reich against the threatening advance of the Allied forces on both fronts.

During those weeks I did not see any of my underground colleagues, and I felt as if events were completely passing me by. I had vaguely heard about a recent Allied landing in France, but its full significance escaped me at the time. Nazi propaganda reinforced general public apathy in playing down the invasion. Accordingly most of us equated it with the disastrous landing at Dieppe in August of 1942.

When I was sufficiently recovered and able to leave the hospital, the news that I had lost my position as governess came as no great surprise. For the past six months, I had repeatedly taken time off to attend to my other activities. Inevitably, this latest and longest absence finally led to my dismissal. I now had plenty of leisure on my hands but little money in my pocket.

I decided that I ought to pay a visit to the Gestapo office, to catch up on any news. I found I had not even been missed, as Frau Bertha had managed to cope with all routine matters without my help. I learned nothing from her, except that Leutnant Boehler was away most of the time on missions and seldom came to the office at all during the day.

About a week later Franz came to see me, as he had heard that I was recovered. We talked about one thing and another. Like so many others in the Resistance, he did not appreciate during those first few weeks that followed D-Day the tremendous strength and overall plan behind the Normandy invasion of June 6. Least of all could anyone anticipate the impact it would have on the outcome of the Second World War.

Franz said he had to talk with me about a recent rescue operation. He had managed to get hold of a list, drawn up by another Gestapo section, that gave the names and addresses of eleven Belgian youths who had been involved in sabotaging German military installations. They had been about to be arrested, and would have been shot or sent to a concentration camp. But Franz had been able to warn them in time, he said, and had even found an empty house, previously occupied by a Jewish family, on the chaussée d'Anvers, where they would be safe. Ten of the youths had now been hiding there for the past forty-eight hours, waiting to be taken to the Namur camp, and thence to a point in one of the French Resistance networks.

"And why are you telling me all this?"

"I need your help."

"I should have guessed. How can I help? There seems to be very little I can do just now."

"On the contrary. You're needed for two main reasons. One is that one man seen repeatedly going in and out of a house that has been empty for such a long time is liable to rouse the neighbours' curiosity. A couple, on the other hand, would not attract special attention. They might live there, or they might be using it as a love nest. The second

reason is that these young men are not used to looking after themselves. They have all lived at home. Cooped up as they are now, they
could stand some female help in keeping the place tidy."

"I suppose you have a point. When do we start?"

"I'll pick you up every day at two in the afternoon. I'll take care of
the supplies, while you clean up and make a list of everything they
may need. The place has to be reasonably well organized."

"How long do you think they can safely stay there, then? It had
better not be too long. Is the Resistance supplying a truck for them?"

"No. I'm looking after that myself. I should be able to get a truck
any day now. By the way, you and I are the only ones who know
about this hide-out. I must insist that you keep it strictly secret."

"Agreed."

"And please don't go there by yourself, under any circumstances. It
would be taking unnecessary risks."

"I understand."

Every day for several days after that we called on the boys at the
house on the chaussée d'Anvers. Franz looked after their material
needs, while I house-cleaned and made friendly small talk. Some of
the boys could not have been older than eighteen. And they seemed to
appreciate my efforts.

Although some "safe" places in occupied territory were never discovered by the Nazis, a prudent agent always had to reckon with the
enemy's vigilance, nosy neighbours, potential informers, traitors, carelessness, and the challenging element of chance. It was probably wise
to assume that a hide-out, however safe, lost some of its safety with
each passing day. That is why, after a whole week had gone by and
there was still no sign of transportation for our fugitives, I began to
worry about their safety.

When I broached the subject with Franz, his answer was evasive.
He said he had tried to get a truck, but there seemed to be a shortage
just now, and the boys would have to be patient a few more days.
Since the Resistance seldom refused to help in such cases, I was at a
loss to understand the delay.

On the following afternoon he did not call to pick me up. I phoned
his apartment but there was no answer. They had not heard from him
at the Gestapo office. Of course it was possible that something had
happened requiring his presence elsewhere. And I knew, after all, the
boys could get along on their own for twenty-four hours. By three
o'clock on the second day, however, when I still did not hear from
Franz, I became restless, and I decided to call on the youths myself.

Their house was a long way from mine, and it took me an hour and a half by trolley-car to reach it. They were there, nervous and worried. They said they were short of a number of things, including soap, which they particularly missed. I promised to bring some of my own; but the other items would have to await my partner's return.

Real soap was one of the scarcer commodities during the war. The ersatz officially sold under that name consisted of a cube of compressed sand and clay, which did not cleanse at all. If anything, it added dirt to the skin. Long ago I had put away two precious cakes of real soap for my own use. I wrapped up one of these and hoped that it would be enough for all ten boys.

On the next day, which was the third of Franz's mysterious absence, I again made the long trip to the chaussée d'Anvers. I was walking towards the house when a middle-aged woman stopped me in the street. She looked agitated, and her voice was high-pitched with alarm: "Madame, please do not go inside that house! The Germans were there last night with a big truck, and pulled out a number of young men! My God! I had no idea there were so many youths in that house! I am a neighbour, Madame. I thought you and your husband lived there alone. I had no idea . . . what a tragedy!"

The shock for me was beyond description. I literally shook where I stood. Choked by emotion, I managed with great difficulty to thank the kindly woman for her warning. I was sure she was a mother herself, for she began to cry with me on the sidewalk. She must have realized, as I did, that all those youngsters were now doomed.

I had been hardened by the war's vicissitudes and steeled by my underground experiences, but this unexpected blow affected me with particular force. It also set me to thinking about Franz. I had known him for a long time—since 1937, which was seven years. We had been friends, co-agents, and underground partners against a common enemy. Yet I had never felt close enough to him to know what made him tick. Maybe a certain youthful immaturity on my part had prevented me from recognizing at first some of his less commendable traits, such as his greed for money. Not being money-minded myself, I had always accepted his excuses for not helping me financially in my hardest times.

Now, too, I recalled that odd evening in May, just before I had fallen ill, when he had invited me to have dinner with him in a small, very chic, and exclusive restaurant, where only the very best food was served. He had said he had some spare money and wished to celebrate. During the Occupation, Brussels saw a number of such small, expensive restaurants, usually with ten tables at most, sprout like mush-rooms and flourish beyond belief. For a small fortune, they offered menus of the highest pre-war standards, prepared from quality foods purchased on the black market. Their patrons, many of whom were German officers, naturally overlooked the fact that such establish-ments were technically illegal.

My host ordered a dinner fit for royalty. We began with caviar on toast and hors d'oeuvres variés, moved on to onion soup, then juicy rib steaks garnished with asparagus and new potatoes smothered in fresh butter, all accompanied by a bottle of fine wine and followed by delicate French pastries, coffee, and liqueurs. I found it hard to believe that there was even a war on and famine in the land. That gastro-nomic feast lulled me into a euphoric mood. But that mood was short-lived.

Franz called for the check, looked at it, and then, showing his Gestapo credentials (he was in mufti), rejected it, stating matter-of-factly, "As a member of the Gestapo, I don't have to pay this." The waiter, dumbfounded, mumbled something about having to call the headwaiter, but he was stopped short by Franz: "Look here, I am with a lady, and I don't want any fuss. If you dare to call anyone, I'll arrest you on the spot."

Completely cowed, the waiter watched us go in silence. I knew the Gestapo, sadistic and ruthless as they were, did not, as a rule, refuse to pay their bills when privately patronizing these establishments. In fact some were even known to be big tippers. This trick of obtaining free meals in expensive restaurants must have been a twist peculiar to Franz.

As we walked away from the table, I quietly asked Franz why the hell he had done that. He replied, unconcerned, "Why not? They're black marketeers and breaking the law; after all, they make enough money."

"But you might at least leave a tip for the waiter."

"Why? I didn't pay the bill, so he doesn't get a tip." He seemed to treat the whole thing as a huge joke.

Enraged, I turned back to the table, where our waiter was still standing, petrified. I thrust into his hand the few francs I had in my purse. It was more a token than a tip, an unspoken condemnation of my companion and an apology on my part. Under normal circum-stances, I would have slapped my escort's face and walked out on him for good. But I swallowed my fury at Franz's behaviour and held my tongue.

Besides spoiling my evening, the incident revealed another dark, unsavoury side of the man I had once looked upon as a good friend, and whose company had seemed so pleasant to me when I had first known him in the distant past, seven years earlier. I tried at the time to analyze his behaviour at the restaurant and mistakenly ascribed it to sheer cussedness, when in truth—as I realized much later—his motivation had really been pure avarice.

When I mentioned the episode later to Jean, he laughed and assured me it was nothing new to him. "Your friend is well known for playing such tricks," he said. "He tried it with me once, but I would have none of it. I ended up footing the bill myself."

While I sat in the trolley-car on my way back from the raided house on chaussée d'Anvers that afternoon, brooding about Franz, I remembered something else that had bothered me even more. Once, several months before, in a moment of rare candour, he had voiced his conviction that the Germans were so much stronger than the Allies that they would almost certainly win the war. I had rebuked him for such negative thoughts, and decided that he was merely suffering from one of those momentary depressions we all knew at times. But I was not so sure any more. Maybe he had really lost faith in the Allies' cause, or in their strength, and now counted on a German victory. Such an assumption would be a very serious flaw in a secret agent, and one that could easily lead to treason.

My personal trust in him had eroded so much over the past year that I now allowed a frightful suspicion to shape in my mind. Since only the two of us had known about the boys' hide-out, who else could have informed the Gestapo of its existence? And why his sudden lengthy absence at such a critical time? Could he really have betrayed his own wards? Stranger things had happened during the war, with so many traitors masquerading as patriots. But I had to admit to myself that my suspicions were unproven; I decided they would not stand the test of common sense. Why would anyone take such risks and make such an effort to help the boys, only to throw them to the wolves a few days later? Suddenly I felt very lonely. I had to talk to someone I could trust about my gnawing doubts.

On an impulse I made an appointment to see Jean, and that evening I told him everything I knew, secret or no secret, about the ten young men. He listened carefully and with obvious growing concern. He had heard nothing of the operation, he said, and he was sure no one else at headquarters had known about it either. What particularly puzzled him was that Franz had never approached him for help with the transportation. When I asked him whether he suspected Franz of actual betrayal, he shrugged. He confessed that he had never fully trusted him. He termed him a sly fox, who seldom let anything slip out about his mysterious missions, claiming that he received his orders direct from London and that these were no one else's business. Instinctively Jean felt only that all was not as it should be where Franz was concerned; but he found it hard to put a finger on it.

I was vastly relieved that he shared my feelings. He promised to ask his chief to set up a Resistance court of inquiry and request that Franz be present to answer a few questions himself. Jean also advised me to be wary of Franz and to avoid him as much as possible. I should even move from my present address if I could. I assured Jean that I was not really that much afraid of Franz, for he knew that if I were caught, he would also be arrested. I certainly could not afford to move, either. When I left Jean, I felt much better, and in a calmer frame of mind.

Franz returned the following day. I confronted him about the events of the last two days and asked him, in my usual blunt way, if by any chance he had had something to do with the boys' arrest. He looked irritated at this and said I was crazy to nurture such ridiculous notions. His sense of affront seemed genuine enough. I asked him if he had any theory of his own on the whole tragedy.

He hadn't the slightest clue, he said, as so many things could have happened. Then he actually reproved me for "blabbering" to Jean about the whole business. I countered that he had only himself to blame, since he had never told me he would leave the boys—and me as well—in the lurch. His unexplained absence was what had aroused my suspicions in the first place. He dismissed the subject by concluding that what was done was done, and there was nothing we could do, except forget the whole unfortunate mess.

A few days later I found a paying job, in the nick of time. I had no money left, even for food, and was too proud to try to borrow, which was perhaps foolish of me. My new job was again as a governess, and again my employer was a baroness. This time my charge was a slightly retarded twelve-year-old girl. The pay was poor, but at least I could again count on one good meal a day. The overall change of pace of the job and the different environment had a soothing effect on my nerves. And so July gradually passed.

As the Allied invasion began to assume more threatening proportions for the German armies, the Nazis, especially those behind the lines, became increasingly vicious, taking out their frustrations on innocent civilians. They arrested and shot people on the slightest provocation, and sometimes for no reason at all. Those Jews who were still at large faced greater danger than ever.

Franz visited me one day to let me know that Mueller was wondering why I had not shown up at the Gestapo for such a long time. He said he had told the chief I had been in poor health; but it might be wise for me to make an appearance there. I did not like the idea and suggested he tell Mueller we had quarrelled, as lovers sometimes do, and that I was sulking. That would get me off the hook for a while longer, I hoped.

Later in the week I met Jean and asked him if he had investigated Franz any further. He told me the Resistance chief had summoned Franz to headquarters and questioned him about the arrest of the ten young men. Franz had given some alibis they were unable to verify, and since they had no concrete evidence of wrongdoing, the case had been dismissed. But as far as he was concerned, Jean said, he did not trust my partner. Then he told me that most of the local Resistance members had gone to France, where the action was; and he advised me to stay off the streets as much as possible, especially in the evenings, and generally to keep a low profile. The Boches were definitely losing ground now and getting nastier by the day. I followed Jean's advice and remained inactive in the underground, concentrating on my new job as governess and awaiting developments.

One late evening about the middle of August, I was hurrying back to my lodgings for dinner when I saw Franz pacing up and down the street in front of the house. He greeted me, all smiles and friendliness: "Long time no see, Olga. Are you still mad at me?"

I told him I did not remember being angry with him; I had simply decided to rest for the time being. He could always tell Mueller I had had a relapse if necessary.

"That isn't really why I came to see you. I just wanted to say goodbye, or au revoir, rather, before I leave."

"Why? Where are you off to now?"

"I'm going on a long and dangerous mission. I may not be coming back." The dramatic statement caught me unawares. I said as long as he had come to say goodbye, we might as well go somewhere for a drink. I could not invite him into my flat on account of my landlady. He asked me to come and sit in his car instead, where we would be less conspicuous to curious neighbours.

I was intrigued by his gentlemanly farewell. He had always been a smooth talker when he chose to be, and now he seemed to be directing all his charm at me. I could not guess why. He heaped all kinds of praise on my head: I had done my clandestine work well; he had the highest regard for me and my integrity. He also felt that I was the only person he could trust implicitly, and this was the reason he had a special favour to ask of me. The flattery pleased me, but his last words considerably dampened its effect.

He now picked up a small parcel he had been holding in his lap. I wondered if perhaps I had been wrong to doubt Franz, as now, for the first time, he had brought me a present. As I watched, he unwrapped a small sturdy metal box that might have been a jewellery box. He carefully handed it to me, explaining that it contained personal papers and his family heirlooms, and that he wanted to leave it with me in trust. If he did not call for it within the next six months, I was to destroy it or throw it in the river, for it would be of no value to anyone else.

The favour seemed a small thing to do, so I agreed to keep the box for him. I took it, shook hands with him, said goodbye, and wished him good luck. Then I returned to my room. I slid the box into the bottom of my wardrobe and promptly forgot all about it. But it was destined to be remembered again, and for a very long time afterwards.

19

Liberation

After fighting a fierce enemy in secret and devious ways for the better part of four years, I spent the last few weeks before the liberation of Brussels in what I can only describe as a state of suspended animation. Like almost everyone in Belgium, I waited with growing impatience for the Allied breakthrough that would drive the enemy out of our country and set us free at long last. Meanwhile, the days dragged interminably on. On Jean's firm advice—which, coming from him, was tantamount to an order—I now avoided both the Resistance and the Gestapo. I continued with my work as governess, which was light and uninspiring, and I had ample time to brood.

Only two events interrupted the monotony of this waiting period. One was the liberation of Paris on August 25, 1944, and its promise of further victories. The other was a happy discovery that set in motion a whole sequence of important consequences.

On the last day of August, while returning home from work, I ran into Louis, another Resistance friend. He exulted with me over the German retreats and the latest Allied advance, and then casually remarked that even the Gestapo had decamped, abandoning their avenue Louise building. I found this hard to believe and asked how he could be so sure. He said he had passed the building that very morning and had not seen the usual sentries outside. This did not prove to me that the Gestapo had really left Brussels. Louis shrugged amiably and suggested that I go there to see for myself. Which is precisely what I intended to do at next daylight. Since I had my permit to enter the premises, I anticipated no difficulties in satisfying my curiosity.

On the following day—which was September 1—around four in the afternoon, I took the avenue Louise trolley-car. I had prepared a plausible excuse for my long absence in case anyone asked awkward questions—first a quarrel with Franz, then a worsening of my heart condition and a long convalescence. By about four-thirty I was walking up to the building. The two sentries who always guarded the entrance were not there, and the massive iron double doors were closed. But not locked.

When I gave one a push, it swung open easily. The hall, usually alive with Gestapo men and the noise of their jackbooted footsteps, was empty and ominously silent. My own footsteps echoed on the tile floors with a cavernous sound. The downstairs offices were all deserted, their doors left wide open. I walked as far as the guardroom at the end of the hall and glanced inside. No one was there. On the table in the middle of the room, however, lying conspicuously open, was a thick file. Curious, I approached the table to have a closer look. I had scanned several pages before I realized that I was staring at a comprehensive list of the names and addresses of all the informers and traitors who had ever been in contact with the Brussels Gestapo. It was an invaluable piece of evidence, and I impulsively grabbed it and ran out. Only later did it occur to me that the register could have been a booby trap.

When I reached the street again, I stood in front of the door and hesitated for a moment, tempted to go back for one last look at the eighth-floor office. For some reason I decided against it, unwilling to push my luck any further. I was well satisfied that the flight of the Gestapo rats was a sure sign that their ship was sinking, and an indication that the liberating armies could not be far away.

Back in my room I compared my own short list of wanted informers with the register I had just appropriated. Every single traitor on my list of suspects was confirmed against the Gestapo's own master list. I was elated with my find, and felt that the day of reckoning for the traitors was drawing near.

On Sunday, September 3, the last of the German troops left the city. All the previous day, endless processions of military vehicles had crowded the roads leading out of the city. Truckload after truckload bristling with armed soldiers passed through the streets, jeered by the populace.

I did not even wait until the last soldier had gone before I began to carry out my own plan. From my list of informers, I picked out the names and domiciles of those I remembered as the worst offenders, over twenty-five of them. I phoned Jean early the same Sunday morning, letting him know that I intended to spend the day visiting traitors, before they had a chance to take legal shelter and use their ill-gotten money to evade their just punishment. I asked him if he could muster a small group of Resistance men willing to help in my round of retribution. Somewhat to my surprise, he readily agreed to send a handful of sturdy boys, ready and willing to accompany me, to a nearby café.

Six or seven strong—I cannot remember exactly—we went from flat to flat, and house to house, and even to some stores as well, catching our criminals off guard. Each was forced to listen to a concise summary of his or her crimes, straight from my master ledger. A good many of them recognized me at once as the Gestapo clerk who had paid them off. When they were ready to grovel in the dirt, contrite and terrified of us, I left the boys to deal with them more thoroughly. Some of the individuals we visited had to spend time in hospital, and this by no means marked the end of their troubles.

As we marched on, I began to feel like an avenging pied piper, for behind me a flock of other men and women gathered to follow us, smelling blood. Somehow they had discovered our self-appointed mission, and they joined us to seek their own revenge. As soon as we had finished dealing with a traitor, they burst into his premises, destroying everything they could find. As we left, we often saw whole pieces of furniture flying out of the window and crashing on the pavement.

Returning from our rounds late that night, we passed several bonfires fed by rubble, much of which had been expensive furniture only that morning. Men and women danced and sang around the flickering fires, inebriated by the miraculous turn of events and large quantities of beer.

That Saturday night marked the end of the four-year occupation of Brussels by German troops, the second such occupation in the span of only one generation. Late Sunday afternoon, September 3, 1944, the first British tanks appeared in the streets of Brussels, soon followed by the bulk of the advancing army. The tumultuous reception by the populace pouring into the streets in their thousands, the wild enthusiasm, the emotional embraces, the showers of gifts and flowers, the kisses, the boys and girls who crowded onto the tanks, the general excitement of old and young—all this has been told and retold a thousand times, and recounted in word and picture more vividly than I could ever hope to convey.

For me it was an emotional anticlimax. Haunted by thoughts of my parents, my husband, and so many others wasting away in the camps, or perhaps dead, I did not feel in the mood for uninhibited rejoicing, even though I was more than grateful for an end to the Nazi oppression. Rather I shared the cautious relief I saw reflected in the pasty face of an old bearded Jew I met that day; he was blinking, half blinded by the daylight, emerging for the first time from the depths of a dark cellar where he had lived in hiding for three long years.

The general carousing continued for another week, eventually abating as life returned to a more normal routine. In the meantime, I had learned that the British high command had established an intelligence section on rue de la Loi, where the various Belgian ministries had been located before the war. As soon as I heard this, I tucked the register firmly under one arm and hurried to that section. I was crisply received by a British Intelligence officer, a Captain Tomkin, who bade me sit down. He spoke fluent French, which was a blessing for me, as I did not speak a word of English in those days. I hefted the big file onto his desk, and said simply, "Pour vous."

He glanced at the list, and then at me. He must have seen a slip of a girl with a wan smile, but triumph in her eyes. He asked where I had obtained it. When I told him, he raised both eyebrows, but made no comment. He simply asked my name and address.

"My name is Olga . . . I mean, Andrée Fiévez. I beg your pardon, after all these years of living under assumed names, I had nearly forgotten my real name. It is Hélène Moszkiewiez."

My answer did not seem to perturb him for he went on formally, "And you say you picked up this file at the Gestapo. Are you quite sure it *was* the Gestapo?"

"Positive. You see, Monsieur, I work for the Resistance. I happened to be passing by the building. I noticed it was empty, walked in, and found this register on the table."

"Do you know the address of the place?"

"Certainly. It's on avenue Louise. If you like, I can show you where it is."

He got up and went to another office. After a while he returned and gave some orders to a sergeant; then he said, "Very well. I'll go with you, and you can show me." He led me to a waiting jeep, where two NCOs of the Royal Engineers joined us, carrying some contraptions that looked like mine-detectors, and we were off.

In front of the avenue Louise building, I jumped off briskly, proud to show them the way in, when one of the sergeants swiftly grabbed my arm, signing to me that I was not to enter. While I waited in the street, he thoroughly checked the entrance with his detector. To my utter amazement he discovered a powerful mine under the floor in the hall, directly behind the front door. "Anyone walking in would definitely be blown up, together with most of the building," Captain Tomkin told me.

"But I walked in here, and out again, just over a week ago, after the Gestapo had left," I insisted. "How do you explain that?" He seemed as mystified as I was, but tried to explain the mystery by suggesting that my small foot might have missed the mine by a fraction of an inch each time. I am not sure that he fully believed my story. Now I can only dismiss the mystery as another lucky break.

The riddle of the mine miracle did not really bother me until years later, when I found time to think carefully about the episode and discuss it with my present husband. We found Captain Tomkin's original theory unlikely. With a little logic we came up with what seemed to be the only reasonable answer. We decided there could be no question that when I entered the building and later left with the register on September 1, I would certainly have stepped on that mine and been blown to pieces—if it had been there. Before abandoning the premises, probably on August 30, the Gestapo must have issued orders to their sappers to mine the entrance and lay booby traps inside. When I first passed through the door at four-thirty on the afternoon of September 1, the men had not yet been able to do their job. They must have done it the same night, or perhaps very early the following morning. Being in an understandable hurry themselves to clear out of town, the sappers must have mined only the entrance, without bothering about the rest. If I had waited until the second, or the third, instead of going there on the first of the month, I would have been killed. Whatever the real explanation, it is undeniably true that I was incredibly lucky.

Captain Tomkin and I waited for over an hour while the NCOs defused the mine and checked the hall for other booby traps. They found none. As soon as we were allowed in, I led Captain Tomkin straight to the guardroom and showed him where I had found the register. There were many more incriminating papers on the same table, which I must have overlooked the first time, and which he now took with him. He declined my offer to show him around the rest of the premises. He would leave that to someone else, he said, once the building had been entirely checked over and declared completely safe. He asked me to accompany him to rue de la Loi again—"to clear up a few points." By then, it was nearly noon and I was supposed to be at work that day by two.

Back at his office, he wanted to know more about my connection with the Gestapo. I told him, and showed him my German identity card and Gestapo Ausweis. He asked me to leave the documents with him, for further checking. I never saw them again.

He proceeded with his interrogation: "What is your code number?"

"Code number? I don't have a code number, not that I know of."

"If you have worked as an agent for us, you must be known by a code number. It seems strange that you don't know anything about it."

"I'm sorry, but Franz never told me I had one."

"Where is this Franz now?"

"I don't know. He left on a special—he said dangerous—mission in August, and I haven't heard from him since."

He coolly asked me to go on with my story. I kept on talking, generally summarizing my activities during the war, without going into many details; but something in the way he listened, repeating to himself in English every so often "fantastic"—one word I understood —suggested to me that he did not believe half of what I said. This irritated me tremendously, and finally drove me to rudeness.

"Look here, Captain, I am under the strong impression that you don't believe me. If you don't, please just say so. After four years of struggle, it is extremely frustrating to feel that I'm talking in vain. This whole business reminds me of the stupid ways of the Boches."

He surveyed me with a faint smile. He was a man in his late thirties, well groomed and obviously cultivated. I could not help wondering if he had been a lawyer before the war.

"Mademoiselle . . . so far you have not given me any concrete proof to support your story. You must understand that we need evidence, or some means of verifying what you are telling me."

"First of all, I am not Mademoiselle, but Madame. My husband was deported to a concentration camp in 1942. So were my parents. And my name is Hélène Moszkiewiez. If you prefer, Hélène for short."

"I am very sorry to hear about your husband and your parents, Madame Hélène. I hope you will see them again soon. But please continue."

"First I think you should make some inquiries about me." I gave him the name of my previous employer, Mme de Herrandt, and also referred him to Jean, of the Resistance in Namur, and René, the chief.

He jotted down the names, and the interrogation was ended. He promised to be in touch with me, and gave me his office phone number. That number, which I made a special point of memorizing, would help me out of a desperate situation a couple of weeks later.

The first interview was followed by two more, when I was notified that I had been duly investigated and my story confirmed by the Resistance, who knew Franz's code number from London. This placed me in the good graces of the section, and I even gained some notoriety on account of my incredible luck, especially with the missed mine.

My luck held again some weeks later, after my last interview with Captain Tomkin, when I very nearly missed being lynched by a small but fierce mob in the neighbourhood of that same accursed building. It was really my fault, as I had no business being there in the first place. Having nothing in particular to do on a clear, crisp autumn afternoon, I had decided to stroll along the avenue, as of old, but this time unfettered by false identities and fears of a lurking enemy. Or so I thought.

I had just passed the vacant Gestapo building and was walking down the next block when someone, sneaking up from behind me, grabbed my arm and gripped it tightly. I immediately whirled around as far as I could, twisting to free myself, to face a grey-haired man of at least sixty, who shouted at me, "What are *you* doing here? Why didn't you go back where you belong?!"

"What do you mean? I belong right here!"

"Oh no, you don't! You're a Boche! You're one of the Gestapo! I know you!"

"You're crazy! I'm Belgian, not German! And I'm not from the Gestapo! Now will you please let me go?"

"You lie, you German bitch! I live right across from the Gestapo, and I recognized you right away! You can't deny it!"

"I assure you you're mistaken. You must have seen someone else who looks like me."

"Not a chance! Why, you even wear the same clothes now as you did then. You can't fool me, you rotten Hun!"

In mounting anger, and to justify his behaviour to passers-by, he yelled loudly to them, as they paused to listen, "I have just caught this Boche woman, who belongs to the Gestapo! I know her!"

All the while he was twisting my arm with greater force. In pain I screamed at him, "You're hurting me! Let go of me, will you? I repeat: I'm Belgian, not German!"

"Hurting you, am I?! What a nerve you Boches have, after all the tortures you swine have inflicted on innocent people!"

A small crowd of about a dozen people had quickly gathered around us. Their attitude, hardly friendly to begin with, soon turned to open hostility when they heard the argument. One of the bystanders voiced the first definite threat: "What are you waiting for? Let's deal with her right now, on the spot. Dirty bitch!"

"Please listen! I am *not* German, and not one of the Gestapo! I work for the British!"

Another excited bystander shouted, "They're all the same, these traitors! As soon as they're caught, they tell you they worked for the Anglais! They think it'll save their skins! Well, I don't buy it! Come on, folks, let's fix her for good!"

That threat appeared very real to me, and I was thoroughly scared. I saw myself being dragged away, torn apart, crippled or pummelled to death by a crowd that was really on my side but did not realize it. The thought that flashed through my mind at that moment was: how unfair such an end would be after I had managed to survive so many terrible dangers all these war years. It was then that I suddenly remembered Captain Tomkin and his phone number.

At the top of my lungs I shrieked, "Listen! I can prove that I worked for the British! For God's sake, will someone please phone rue de la Loi, and ask to speak to Captain Tomkin of British Intelligence!" I shouted the phone number.

The mob's mood had risen to such a pitch that they ignored my plea. Only one well-dressed woman at the periphery of the crowd calmly suggested that they call: "After all, we'll soon know whether she's lying or not. I don't think it's right to take the law into our own hands." She spoke in a cultivated voice and seemed to inspire some respect in my other attackers. After some further discussion, she was allowed to go to phone. I repeated the number for her several times and waited, panting, as the crowd held me. After about five minutes, she returned and announced, looking puzzled, that she had indeed spoken to a Captain Tomkin, who said he was coming right away; he asked that they be patient and do nothing until his arrival.

Meanwhile the old man was holding the crowd's attention by telling them that, being retired, he had spent many long hours watching the comings and goings at the Gestapo across the street, and that he had often seen me freely entering and leaving the place, sometimes with Gestapo officers. Perhaps unwittingly he was adding fuel to a smouldering fire, which made me feel even more vulnerable.

It took Captain Tomkin an eternal thirty minutes to appear. He hailed me right away. "Madame Hélène! What the dickens are you doing in this neighbourhood?" After I had given an account of myself, he turned to the fascinated crowd. "This lady here is known to me. She is certainly not a friend of the Germans. She did not work *for* the Gestapo. She worked *at* the Gestapo, but as a secret agent, for the Allied cause."

His audience stood gaping in silent amazement. It would not have surprised me to learn that some of the bystanders had gone away disappointed to have missed the chance to beat me up. The man who had originally grabbed and held me was the most embarrassed. He apologized to me profusely, said he was terribly sorry to have caused me such anguish, and admitted he had been unfair to jump to conclusions. He confessed it had never crossed his mind that any man, or woman, *could* penetrate the Gestapo as an agent. He praised me for my courage, until it was my turn to feel embarrassed. I admitted that in his place I would probably have done the same thing. He invited me to have coffee with him at his home across the street, as he very much wanted to introduce me to his wife. I had to politely decline his invitation, as I was still slightly shaken and only wanted the captain to take me home.

The well-dressed woman, who had not left when the crowd dispersed, came over to me, shook my hand, and admitted, smiling, that she had not believed me at first either, and had thought that the phone number was just a ploy to gain time. She was very relieved to have been wrong in her first assumption.

While Captain Tomkin was driving me home, he firmly warned me to keep away from that sector of town, since others might also recognize me as a Gestapo employee and not wait for explanations. He was right, of course. It had been a very close call indeed.

20

Pandora's Box

Looking into my wartime past, I am intrigued to recognize many connections between incidents that, at the time, seemed insignificant. Only now can I appreciate the chain of events that produced such dramatic results and the decisions that determined the future course of my life. The story of the jewellery box entrusted to me by Franz is a perfect example of that kind of domino effect.

Following the Liberation there were still pockets of Germans in the city, too slow, or reluctant, or incredulous of the German defeat, to leave Brussels. Groups like these were common throughout Europe at the time. Within several weeks of the triumphant entry of the British Twenty-first Army into Brussels, a member of the Resistance reported to Jean that a party of German men and women was still hiding in an isolated basement under the university complex, which was closed at the time.

Jean alerted the British authorities, who immediately provided a truck and soldiers to flush out this passive pocket of Teutonic tenacity. He asked me if I wanted to go along as interpreter, with the added duty, if it proved to be necessary, of handling the women. Always pleased to help, and curious, I accepted the offer with alacrity.

With the Tommies we burst into the hide-out, ready for anything. All we found were a few weary Blitzmädchen in poor condition, a handful of unarmed soldiers, and several men in civilian clothes, in all some twenty-five remnants of Hitler's Reich, surrounded by enough provisions to last for many months. I suppose they were awaiting the return—or perhaps the Second Coming—of the German forces. What startled me most that afternoon, however, was the sight of a familiar face among the civilians. Fortunately Mueller did not see me. I quietly identified him to Jean, who turned me around and pushed me outside without a moment's hesitation. "Don't let him see you. For security's sake, it would be better if you didn't show your face to him. Actually, I don't think you'll be needed here any more. Be a good girl and wait for me in my car. I won't be long." I had always respected Jean's decisions and so obeyed without question.

Less than half an hour later, he rejoined me. In high spirits, he recounted how the Boches had been taken away and treated as prisoners of war, a far kinder fate than would have befallen the fugitives had the nationalities been reversed. Then, changing the subject, he said: "Since you've been so patient, I am inviting you out for dinner. What do you say?" The noontime meal, of course, was the main repast of the day. I accepted with pleasure, but pointed out that I could not possibly go dressed as I was. I would have to fix my hair and fetch my coat, if he did not mind driving me home and waiting for me. It would take me only a few minutes to get ready.

On the way there, while chatting about one thing and another, Jean mentioned Franz: "If he's not turned up by now, he's probably not alive any more. Might have been caught, tortured, shot. Who knows?" The idea made me feel a little guilty for having lost faith in the man. When we got out of the car, Jean followed me to my room, to ensure, he said good-naturedly, that I hurried. Upstairs I rummaged for my good shoes in the bottom of my wardrobe. Underneath them was Franz's metal box, which I had completely forgotten in all the excitement of the Liberation. While I put my shoes on, I said to Jean, "Apropos of Franz, I still have that box of his. It'd completely slipped my mind."

Jean, suddenly alert, asked, "What box? What the hell are you talking about?!"

"Sorry, didn't I tell you? He asked me to hold onto a box, the one over there in the wardrobe. He told me there are family heirlooms and some private papers in it. If he doesn't come back for it within six months, I'm supposed to destroy it, or throw it in the river. That's what he said." Jean remained thoughtfully silent. He finally asked when Franz had given it to me. I said the middle of August.

"Strange. Very curious. Why six months? He should have been back by now. I don't like that; I don't like it at all. I smell a rat, Olga. Let's open that box now and see what's inside."

"I really don't think we should, Jean. He left it to me in trust. What it contains is none of our business. We'd be prying . . ."

"Prying, my foot. I'm surprised a smart girl like you could be so naïve. Who would want his family heirlooms thrown away?"

"Well, even if you're right, what does it have to do with us?"

"The more I think about it, the less I like it. Listen, I'll take the responsibility for opening it."

"But I don't have the key."

"No problem. A friend of mine is a locksmith. He lives near here. He'll have a key that will fit. Let's take the box and go there right now, before we eat."

The locksmith could not, after all, find a satisfactory key, and he told us the lock would be a complicated one to pick. Over my weak protestations, Jean ordered him to force the lid open; so a few minutes later we were both peering into the box, with what I then considered reprehensible curiosity.

There were no recognizable heirlooms inside. There were only documents. Jean glanced through some of them quickly, then let out a low whistle of astonishment. Wordlessly he passed a few papers to me. They were recent title deeds, in Franz's real name, for three properties in Paris, two for apartment buildings and one for a twenty-room hotel.

"This real estate is worth millions, even at present low prices. Where the hell did he get that much money? He always complained he was so short of cash, remember?"

I remembered only too well. I also began to suspect why he had been so secretive about his many "missions"; but I still could not guess how he had managed to accumulate enough capital to invest in such properties.

The rest of the papers were in German, so Jean asked me to translate them for him. However, given my scant knowledge of the written language, especially official or legal German, I could decipher only a word here and there, and some figures. The seals indicated that they had been issued by some German military authority, like the Abwehr. Jean looked at them again and said that he smelled treason. "Olga, I think you'd better take that box and its contents to the British authorities just as they are. The sooner the better. There is definitely something wrong there."

"All right. But on one condition, Jean: that you come with me. I'm a bit nervous about going alone."

"Fine. I'll go with you first thing tomorrow."

We ate a late lunch that day, and a less happy one than we had anticipated.

Early the following morning, we called on the intelligence section on rue de la Loi. We were received by a Major Harris, who was replacing Captain Tomkin. The major was a man of about forty; he spoke flawless French without a trace of an accent. I handed over the box, explaining the circumstances under which it had been entrusted to me and how, at Jean's insistence, we had decided to pry it open and check its contents.

The officer listened politely, but with a slightly bored look. He finally glanced through the papers himself. When I saw him scratch his head, I knew he could not read German. He excused himself, went to another office, and returned with two more officers. One of them sat down in one corner of the room to read the documents. While we waited, I told Major Harris my name and aliases. I said that I was well known to Captain Tomkin, who must surely have assembled a file on me. The major called for my file. After perusing it, he said, with a smile, "Yes, I remember. You are the girl who worked for the Gestapo and were nearly blown up by a mine there." I smiled at the definition.

The translator finished his work and called to his colleagues. They conferred briefly in hushed voices, and the major came back to his desk. His smile had now vanished, and he looked grave when he spoke. "I am afraid this is very serious. Very serious indeed. Did you read these papers?"

"Only the deeds in French, sir. Not the German ones, as I couldn't understand them very well."

He leaned back in his chair and observed me as if he had not really seen me before. "Let's clarify a few matters now. You say you worked in a Gestapo office. Did they speak German there?"

"Of course. Nothing but."

"Then you do know German, don't you?"

"Yes, I can speak it fluently and without an accent, but I've never learned to write it or to read anything as difficult as these documents. I should explain that I worked there as an assistant to Franz, your agent, and so I wasn't required to write."

"That seems rather incredible. Suppose some officer there had asked you to write a letter, for example, in German? What would you have done?"

"Oh! But some officers did ask me. I told them it was not my job, since I worked as an unpaid volunteer. I told them they should have it done by one of their regular secretaries. In one case I acted angry and left the room, slamming the door."

He considered me for a moment and smiled slightly. "Yes, I think you would. But I have to ask you a few more questions."

The ensuing interrogation was thorough and tiring, and lasted all day. He wanted to know everything about me: how long I had known Franz, what kind of work he had made me do, what our real relationship had been, whether or not I had had sexual intercourse with him (I was glad I could truthfully say no to that), where I had worked, what I had done in my spare time, and so on. It slowly dawned on me that I was in the dock, not Franz. Jean, sitting next to me, must have had the same impression, for he interrupted my questioner abruptly: "If you suspect *her,* you're barking up the wrong tree! After all the work she's done for you, the Anglais, and for the whole Resistance, I find it outrageous that you would subject her to such questioning! Why on earth would she have brought you such incriminating documents if she were a traitor?"

The major remained calm and unruffled by the outburst. In measured words he replied, "This means nothing. And I am not accusing her of anything. But in a case as serious as this, we must have all the facts established beyond any reasonable doubt. Anyway, it is now lunch-time so we shall have a short recess. I shall expect you back here in about an hour's time."

Jean was seething, and he vented his indignation during our meal. "I am so sorry, Olga, to have got you into all this trouble. If I'd known that you would be placed under suspicion and would have to answer a lot of ridiculous questions, I would never have asked you to take that damned box to them. To hell with the Anglais!"

Personally I did not feel threatened by the interrogation, which I understood as merely a necessary part of the officer's duties. Perhaps Jean, though, who had had more experience in these matters, feared I might fall victim to the petty bureaucratic bumbling of the military.

After lunch the questioning continued. "Now about Franz. As you know, he is one of our registered agents. And so, we have verified, are you. Have you seen him at all since he gave you that box?"

"No, and I haven't the slightest idea where he is—if he's still alive."

"Have you been to his lodgings?"

"Yes, but his landlady said that he's been away since the middle of August and she hasn't heard from him since."

"Did you ever have any suspicions about his activities before this? What I mean is, have you ever suspected him of working for the Germans as well as for us?"

I hesitated momentarily. "All I know is that for the past year or so, he was very secretive about himself, especially about his missions and absences. Yes, occasionally I did suspect him of something, but I was never able to put my finger on anything concrete." I described the Gestapo arrest of the ten young men hiding at chaussée d'Anvers, and my doubts then about Franz's part in the raid. However, it is difficult to convey instinctual feelings to another person. The major listened carefully, but did not seem to think my suspicions well founded. But he kept probing.

"You were a registered agent. Why did you have to work as a governess?"

"That is quite simple, Major. I had to survive, that's why. I have no money of my own, you know."

"Franz did not pay you a monthly stipend, then? And provide you with ration cards and food stamps?"

I laughed bitterly. "Franz pay me? What a joke! I never saw a single cent from him. The few times I did ask for financial help, he complained of being short of cash himself and said he didn't receive any money from London. I never received a single ration card, or even a food stamp, from him."

Here Jean intervened once more: "I can vouch for that. I know Franz always complained of not getting funds from London, and I know Olga—I mean, Hélène—was broke most of the time."

The major looked annoyed at the interruption. "Monsieur, I don't know you. You may be from the Resistance movement, but so are thousands of others. Whatever you may have to say does not affect these proceedings. Please don't interrupt."

I could see that Jean was making a supreme effort to control his temper. "Very well," he replied stiffly, "In that case I will call on René, our chief, to come up here and testify for Olga. I am sure you must know René."

"That would be most helpful. Thank you." He turned back to me. "Madame Hélène, I think that will be all for today. You may go now." Then he added, in a slightly threatening tone, "I must warn you not to move from your present address, as you may be called by us at any time. Is that understood?" I said I understood, but I went away with a bitter taste in my mouth, wondering what I had done wrong.

Jean, true to his word, persuaded René, chief of his Resistance group, to come all the way from Namur to testify in my favour. I considered his support more than kind as I did not officially belong to his flock. I had always depended on Franz, who had depended on London, though we both operated with the help of the Resistance.

Two days after the first interrogation, Jean, René, and I were back at rue de la Loi. René was well known to that section of British Intelligence, and his word carried weight. His strong testimony in my favour did much to dispel the major's earlier reservations as to my loyalties. Major Harris, now more relaxed with us, disclosed that the documents found in Franz's box left no doubt whatsoever that Franz had been a double agent. He also clarified some other points.

"I have checked with London, and I can assure you that Franz received sufficient funds from us to ensure payment of your monthly stipend in full. We also supplied him, over the years, with a fairly large number of ration cards and stamps for distribution where and when needed." He paused to note my reaction of astounded silence before continuing: "Our agents are not supposed to work for a living, unless as a cover. With what we pay them, they can live decently in comfort, if not in luxury, without having to seek other employment. That is why I was surprised to learn that you were obliged to work for a living."

The news that I had been a registered agent in the pay of British Intelligence stunned me. Franz had obviously found it more profitable to keep me in the dark. While I had scraped and scrounged, skirting starvation month after month, year in and year out, he had deliberately pocketed my pay and sold my ration stamps on the black market.

The major waited for me to say something. I said what I thought was obvious: "You understand, I hope, that if I had not been burdened with money problems and the restrictions of a job, I could have done more, much more, and far better work for you. Franz must surely have known it, but didn't care. What a pity."

"I know. But you will be interested to hear that we have now issued a warrant for his arrest. We have a fairly good idea where he can be found. I will advise you as soon as we find him. Meanwhile, do keep in touch."

Franz was arrested ten days later in Paris, together with his Belgian mistress. I hadn't even known he had a mistress. The day after he was brought back to Brussels, two officers called at my apartment and asked me to accompany them to rue de la Loi for the routine confrontation.

When I saw him in the office, he was as cool and composed as always. Major Harris presided and asked the questions. "Madame Hélène Moszkiewiez, do you know this man?"

"Of course I do. Hullo, Franz. So you are alive after all?" He did not answer.

"Monsieur François Vermolen, do you know this woman?"

"I do."

Jean was brought in and was asked the same question; but, being Jean, he could not suppress a sarcastic comment: "Alors, mon vieux, you've had a rip-roaring time in Paris?" He received no answer.

His mistress, a tall, slightly plump brunette with no distinctive features, followed him. We had never seen each other before. Jean did not know her either.

Then the major produced the jewellery box. This took Franz completely by surprise, as he had not been told that it and its contents were in the hands of the British authorities.

"Monsieur François Vermolen, do you recognize this box and the documents in it?"

"I do." His overall self-control was remarkable, but he could not help casting an angry glance at me and spitting out once in my direction, "You bitch!"

"Don't congratulate me," I answered with calm sarcasm. "Jean is the one who suspected you all along and ordered that the box be opened and brought here."

The confrontation was over. Franz was taken away, and Jean and I were free to go. Although I would see Jean occasionally after our confrontation with Franz, this was the last of our Resistance work together. I do not know where he is today.

When I saw Major Harris again some days later, he informed me that Franz, who was in prison awaiting trial, had testified that I knew absolutely nothing about his treasonable activities, and that my work for the underground had always been above reproach. This at least cleared away any doubts lingering in the major's mind. I requested permission, which was granted, to visit the prisoner.

I had many questions about this man, whom I had first met when I was a young sixteen-year-old and he, a witty, sophisticated, cheerful young lieutenant of twenty-five, the same man with whom I had plotted and connived against the Nazis for four oppressive war years; who had swindled me of my pay, knowing all the time of my penury while he accumulated a good-sized fortune; who had sold my share of rations, knowing of my hunger; and who, in the end, had been exposed as a double agent and traitor to his country. Although I had finally accepted that he was obsessively greedy for wealth, I still could not bring myself to believe that the lust for money was capable of so completely destroying a man's soul and dignity. I intended to find out if I could.

He greeted me without any visible emotion, and we exchanged a few banalities. I thanked him for having at least told the truth about me at his interrogation. He made an unexpected comment: "That was a dirty trick you played on me."

"You know very well how it happened. It was out of my hands, anyway. But what puzzles me is this: why did you do what you did?"

"It's too complicated to explain. You wouldn't understand."

I did not know what he meant, but decided not to press for an explanation. "Well, what about my monthly salary, which you simply pocketed yourself? And those ration stamps I never saw? Is that too complicated for me to understand as well?"

"I didn't receive any extra funds for you. I don't care what London says."

I did not believe him. On an impulse, I broached another subject that had been nagging me for a long time. "Listen, François, obviously it doesn't matter any more, but just to satisfy my curiosity, tell me: you did turn in those ten young men, didn't you?"

He thought for a moment, as if trying to remember. "What young men? When?"

"You know, the ten young men you were hiding in that empty house on the chaussée d'Anvers, and who were arrested while you were away?"

"Oh! Now I remember. Those guys. Yes, of course. I had to."

"Why?"

With some irritation he replied, "Why? Because Mueller was after me! I hadn't done anything for the Gestapo for a long time. I had to show some results, didn't I?"

"Granted. But why sacrifice *ten* boys, when one, or even two, would have been more than enough?"

"Well, ten looked better than one or two. Anyway, that's all water under the bridge now."

Now my questions had been answered as far as François would answer them. I was appalled by the dehumanizing effect Gestapo work had had on his character. As to whether the Franz I had known had ever really existed, I did not know. Surely I no longer recognized him in this man. I felt like spitting in his face and left abruptly, disgusted. I had no wish ever to see him again. And I never did.

Two years later, when I came back to Belgium from abroad after some eighteen months' absence, I was shopping in a Brussels department store when a plump young woman greeted me. I could not place her, though I vaguely remembered having seen her somewhere before. She said cheerfully, "Don't you remember me? We met at rue de la Loi, with that English major." She was François's mistress.

"Now I remember! And how are you?"

"I am fine, thank you. The authorities had nothing against me."

"What about François?"

She looked at me with surprise. "Haven't you read the newspapers?"

"I'm afraid not. You see, I've been abroad since 1946, when François was still waiting for his trial."

"Bad news," she shrugged casually. "He was tried here, but the British military authorities weren't satisfied with the sentence, so they appealed. He was extradited and tried in England, found guilty of treason, and sentenced to death. He was hanged."

Her indifference disturbed me. "And what about yourself?"

She replied she was living with her mother and her two children, whom she had had by Franz. He had promised to marry her but, in view of what had eventually happened, she thought it was just as well he hadn't. She simply seemed to be a placid sort of woman who accepted her lot philosophically. She said she was planning to be married soon.

That was all I ever heard about Franz. He undoubtedly deserved his fate. But had I not taken part in flushing out those hidden Germans that day, recognized Mueller, and earned Jean's spontaneous lunch invitation, I would not have been foraging for my new shoes, incidentally noticing the jewellery box in the wardrobe and mentioning it to Jean, with the resulting consequences. The chances are that I would have faithfully returned it to Franz, unopened, if he had called for it before the end of the six months. And I wonder, too, if perhaps the revelations of Franz's treason might have surfaced in some other way.

Epilogue

After September 1944 we were rid of the Nazis' evil presence, but not of their final destructiveness. V1s, dubbed "doodle-bugs", and the treacherous V2 rockets continued to plague us throughout the fall and winter of that year, killing many innocent civilians and randomly destroying property. The population of Brussels, like that of Antwerp, London and other places, withstood the final thrashing of the ailing Nazi dragon with philosophical fortitude.

A last whiff of the dying monster's putrid breath drifted over Belgium at Christmas of 1944 and New Year's of 1945, during the German counter-offensive in the Ardennes, a mere forty miles from Brussels. Those were days of crushing anxiety, particularly for the surviving Jews, who were haunted by the nightmarish prospect of new terrors and tortures, should the Boches return. But the Battle of the Bulge was won in January of 1945, and the enemy thrown back. We could start to breathe again.

Even after its extermination, the Nazi dragon was able to horrify us with the extent of its evil. From the recently liberated concentration camps emerged some of the skeletal survivors who were slowly trickling back through the Red Cross reception centres. They returned with stories of incredible suffering and horrors, and they also brought back news of those who had perished in the Holocaust. Among those who did not return were my mother, my father, Albert, my husband of a few days, and many, many friends.

With anxious crowds of people who had relatives or friends in concentration camps, I spent many hours at the local reception centre, as did my sister and her husband, trying to glean scraps of news about our parents and relatives, and looking for surviving friends.

One of the first survivors that I recognized was Ruthie Calanos. Ruthie and I had been through school together; we had been inseparable friends. I remembered her as a girl of striking beauty, with jet black hair and dark brown eyes set in a perfectly oval face. She was a jovial and carefree girl with a small sensual mouth and pearly white teeth that showed when she laughed. Her parents were Greek Sephardic Jews and had raised her in their strict orthodox ways. At the age of sixteen she was still completely innocent in sexual matters. One day she had confided to me, with alarm, that she might be pregnant. Greatly shocked, I asked, "How did you let this happen?"

"Well, you know Maurice—" he was a common friend "—last night he kissed me on the mouth."

"And then?"

"That's all."

"You mean, all he did was kiss you on the mouth? Nothing else?"

"No. Why?"

Accordingly I had felt a responsibility to tell Ruthie the facts of life, which I had done. In 1942 or 1943, when the Gestapo picked her up with her parents, she was still a virgin. In the twenty endless months that followed, she was used and abused, day after day, by dozens of SS swine, who kept her in a camp brothel.

When I saw her that day at the reception centre in 1945, she was a stone-faced, silent, and neurotically depressed wreck of only twenty-three years. After those two hellish years she cringed at the mere sight of a man. Her parents never returned, so Ruthie was completely alone in the world. I took her home with me for a few days until she could be admitted to an institution. There she underwent psychiatric treatment for about six months. Eventually she got married and had three children; but she died young, of cancer of the cervix, which I attribute directly to her ordeal at the hands of those SS criminals.

On another day, at the same centre, I was hailed by a dwarf-like, shrivelled old man. "Hélène! How are you? I see you don't recognize me. I'm Moses, your pal from the Gordonia. Remember?"

The Moses I remembered from a Zionist organization we had both been involved with had been a strapping young fellow, tall and handsome, and bursting with health and vigour. I could not see any resemblance between that Moses and this frail dwarf before me, except for his eyes and some briefly familiar facial expressions as he spoke. He had been one of the many human guinea pigs for the degenerate Dr. Mengele's inhuman experiments and had somehow survived, a living sample of that monster's atrocities.

There were also some miraculous reunions, such as that of my uncle Bernard, his wife, and their two sons, my cousins. Each of the four had been sent to a different concentration camp, and all had somehow returned alive. But cases like these were, of course, rare.

Brussels did not take too long to recover from the mournful years of Nazi domination and to regain its international reputation as a city of gaiety. Its well-stocked shops, superb restaurants, theatres, and cabarets, and general amenities, together with the Rabelaisian cheerfulness of its citizens, attracted soldiers on furlough in ever larger numbers. In those happier years Brussels competed with friendly Copenhagen as a city of "good times".

With the Liberation there was naturally no more work for me in the Resistance. I was tired of working for a pittance, so I resigned my position as governess to look for more profitable employment. Finally cutting my tenuous ties with the nobility, I applied for a commoner's job with the NAAFI, which hired me. The Navy, Army, and Air Force Institute was the official caterer to the thousands of British and other Allied troops stationed in and around Brussels, as they passed through or arrived on leave. The NAAFI facilities were in a large building on boulevard Botanique, directly in front of the botanical gardens.

Fortunately, my duties there did not require any knowledge of English, as I was hired to sell candy to the troops. For the first time in four years I enjoyed a decent wage, as well as an avalanche of tips, for soldiers on leave are generous. But I felt lonelier there than I had ever been before, lost among crowds of boisterous soldiers, whose language I could not understand and whose high spirits, jokes, and gestures meant little to me. A small army of local waitresses attended these herds of hungry and thirsty men (we could serve only tea or coffee to quench their thirst). The waitresses were really my co-workers, but I found them generally coarse, promiscuous girls, ready to go to bed with any soldier at the drop of a few banknotes.

One evening in October of 1944 a British soldier sitting all by himself at a small table called me over and wanted to know if I worked there as a volunteer. Surprised at the question, and without thinking, I answered rather heatedly: "A volunteer? After starving all these years? No way, thank you very much!" He smiled and said he admired my frankness. I was about to turn away when it suddenly struck me that he had been speaking fluent French with no accent. I turned around and said, as if I had just made a discovery, "Mais vous parlez français!" He laughed and asked if I were free after work to show him around Brussels, as he did not know the town very well. I had a second look at the man. He seemed quiet and serious, and reminded me in a vague, indefinable way of my father. I apologized, but said I worked the evening shift until eleven, a little late for sightseeing. He did not insist.

Later that evening, in my room, I thought about the French-speaking soldier. I regretted that I had not spoken with him longer, as I felt we could have enjoyed a pleasant conversation. I realized, with some sadness, that I would probably never see him again, as so many chance encounters during those years were brief and not repeated. On the following evening, to my delight, he was there, sitting at the same table. I greeted him and he seemed genuinely glad to see me. I reminded myself that he was probably as lonesome as I was. We chatted for a few minutes, and he asked me again when I would be free to show him the sights. I said I finished work at four that Wednesday afternoon, the next day, if he could make it. He said he could. His name was Albert—another Albert, but much older than my late husband would have been.

Only when we had been out a couple of times did I discover that Albert knew Brussels better than I did. "You tricked me," I said, pretending an indignation I could not feel. He admitted it had been an innocent ploy to arrange a date with me. He had been brought up in Brussels, he confessed, though he had been born in England. He lived in South America, had joined the British armed forces as an overseas volunteer, and had been assigned to a special intelligence unit (the top-secret M16, as I learned much later).

"And why did you ask me if I was a volunteer worker at the NAAFI? It seemed to be such a stupid question to ask. Or was that another one of your ploys?"

"Maybe. Actually, you didn't seem to belong with all those other wild wenches. I thought you were probably some girl of the bourgeoisie doing her patriotic duty for king and country by looking after the welfare of us poor heroes. You looked so frail."

"The way you put it, it sounds like a compliment. Anyway, you're forgiven."

I would not presume to explain the chemistry of mutual attraction between two human beings. I only know that Albert and I were strongly drawn to each other from the beginning. As our relationship grew, I gradually told him about my parents, my late husband, and my wartime adventures. He was a good listener, and a sympathetic one. My story fascinated him, and especially my connection with the Gestapo, which he thought would make a good book one day. Eventually I also told him I was Jewish. To my surprise, he said he had guessed as much, and in fact his own background was Jewish as well!

Early in 1945 Franz was still incarcerated, pending his trial, when Major Harris called for me and made me a surprising offer. Would I consider continuing to work as an agent for British Intelligence on a special mission in the near future? My job would be to unearth a number of war criminals, former Gestapo officials, SS officers, and so on, who were still known to be at large in occupied Germany. British Intelligence would need my help in arresting them and bringing them to trial. I would have officer status as an undercover agent, receiving a very generous salary, and all my expenses would be paid—lodgings, car, and chauffeur. It was an attractive and flattering offer, and I said so.

The major commented, "We think you have the right personality and motivation for this kind of work. That is why we are offering you this mission." He was persuasive, but my acceptance would have meant I would be spending most of my time in Germany, a country I had come to loathe. I asked the major if I had to give an answer right away; I would need to give the offer very careful thought. He gave me a couple of weeks.

In the meantime, Al and I became much closer. We continued to find we had a great deal in common, and we now spent most of our free time together. One day he told me he was being posted to Germany for a while. In a few months' time he would be demobilized and would return to South America, to his original job as an accountant. He confessed he was very fond of me—he did not want to use the word "love", which he claimed had been corrupted beyond all meaning—and would I care to marry him? He did not want to rush me, he said, but he would expect an answer when he came back to Brussels on furlough. The day he left for Germany, I knew what my answer would be.

Two weeks later I returned to see Major Harris. I told him, quite openly, that I was considering marriage and needed much more time to reach my final decision. He did not seem to take my matrimonial intentions too seriously: "You should bear in mind, of course, that you will be called as a witness at François Vermolen's trial."

"When will that be?"

"In six or seven months, perhaps later."

"But what if I accept your offer to go to Germany? I won't be here then."

"There would be no problem. You would simply be recalled for a few days, that's all."

"And if I decide to get married and leave for America with my husband several months before the trial, what happens then?"

My question implied that I might refuse the organization's attractive offer. I wanted to keep my options open until I received further news from Albert, for the war was still on and he, like my first Albert, might not come back. The major understood what I was doing, and his former gentle manner gave way to a mild form of verbal blackmail. "You must realize that if you attend the trial, you will receive all the back pay to which you have been entitled since 1942. A considerable sum, you know. And you would be recommended for a decoration."

"Meaning that if I don't attend the trial, I lose all those benefits? Even the decoration?"

"I'm afraid so."

I did not mince words in letting him know how I felt. If a decoration was going to depend on such trivialities, I said, then I did not want it. As for the money—well, I had managed to survive without it all these years and could survive without it again. He seemed taken aback by my reaction and retreated behind bureaucratic excuses, saying it did not really depend on him whether I was recompensed or not. That was for the court to decide. Regarding the decoration, there were certain rules and certain channels that were not within his jurisdiction. "However," he added to placate me, "I expect you will receive some form of acknowledgement for services rendered, in any case." (In time I did receive a standard Certificate of Service, signed by Field Marshal Montgomery.) At this point the major finally accepted a compromise. He would expect a definite answer from me within a month.

Almost immediately after this last interview, I began to receive letters from Albert every few days. In the most recent one, some two weeks after the talk with Major Harris, he announced triumphantly that he had managed to have himself posted back to Brussels, and would arrive in a few days, complete with a newly acquired dachshund for me. Her name was Lottie, and he had paid forty cigarettes for her. She became a very dear companion, travelling all over the world with me; she died at the ripe old age of fifteen in Vancouver.

The evening before I gave my final answer to Major Harris, I made my decision. I mulled over the many changes in my life, including the many disasters I had so narrowly missed. I remembered the constant hunger and privation, and my constant fear of arrest by the Gestapo. I had had little opportunity or inclination for romance during those dark, bleak days. Now I compared those years to my present possibilities. I had found a man I loved, and who loved me, and I was now asked to give him up to chase Nazi war criminals all over their own territory. That choice would mean another fake identity, new impersonations, more loneliness, and the kind of double life I had thought I had left behind for good. Much as I would have liked to catch a few SS and Gestapo criminals and see them hanged, I was not willing to gamble away my own happiness on their account. As for the money and the status, their lure had never been very strong for me, and they were definitely not strong enough now to alter my decision to marry Albert. Even as I tried to weigh my choices, I knew I would go with him wherever he went. For me the war was over.

The disappointed major expressed his regret, but said he still hoped I would change my mind. In the end he had to be satisfied with my written affidavit in lieu of verbal testimony at François's trial.

I told Albert my decision when he came back, and soon afterwards we were married. When he went to Aldershot, England, for demobilization, I was allowed to wait for him in London, in my new status as the war bride of a South American volunteer. I spent the waiting months at the Hyde Park Crescent address of South American House, trying to learn English. Albert joined me there, and in 1946 we sailed for a new world with Lottie.

Now, so many years later, I can say I never regretted that decision to follow the dictates of my heart.